Ted Williams: 'Hey kid, just get it over the plate!'

Ted Williams: 'Hey kid, just get it over the plate!'

A book about Baseball's Golden Age, its great players and twinkling stars

By Russ Kemmerer with W.C. Madden

Library of Congress Card Number: 2002114501

Copyright 2002 by Russ Kemmerer
ISBN 0-9645819-3-0

Published by Madden Publishing Co., Inc.
10872 Washington Bay Drive
Fishers, IN 46038

For all general information contact Madden Publishing at:
317-842-9856
wmadden@peoplepc.com
www.baseballstoriesforthesoul.homestead.com

Photos courtesy of Brace Photo, Topps and Russell D. Kemmerer.

Dedication

This journal is dedicated to my sons Russell Dean and Darrel James; my daughters Cheryl and Kimberly, my own whom I love; and to their own, Matt, Molly, Jami, Adam, Tyler, Lea, Robin, Ryan, Joshua, and Brooke, whom I also love dearly.

I equally dedicate this book to Susannah K. Kemmerer, my wife, companion, friend, bouncing board, and chief advisor, whom I love beyond words. Without her undying support, understanding, endless encouragement, and patience this journal never would have been written.

4

Contents

Acknowledgments

I want to acknowledge Richard Sanderson, editor in his own right, high school friend and teammate, who encouraged, guided, emphasized his presence in humor as only he can bring it to reality and who spent numerous hours with me on the telephone discussing ideas and suggestions that came to reality on these pages.Also Jane Miller, my former teaching associate, who gave of her valuable time to edit and add her expertise to the writing.

And I could never forget the help and encouragement I received from countless friends, former teammates, major league players, companions who lived the life and experiences it with me and added flavor and a taste of the game for all those who still believe that baseball is the greatest game ever played on earth.

Foreword

T ed Williams: *"Hey kid, just get it over the plate!"* is a descriptive and colorful chronicle of baseball's golden days. Russ Kemmerer gives an inside perspective into the lives of many of baseballs most influential sports heroes, from Ted Williams to Walt Dropo. The reader is provided with a unique view of these memorable times, historic ballparks, unparalleled fans loyalty and support that lived and died with their teams and heroes in good times and bad.

The story spans Kemmerer's entrance into professional baseball and his journey through nine years and four major league teams, Boston Red Sox, Washington Senators, Chicago White Sox, and Houston Astros. Not only does he describe the intricacies of the game, the personal relationships that remain intact through passing time, but the players passion to simply put on their uniforms, tie their shoes, tug their caps, and walk out onto the fields to play the game. It was not the money that drove them, but the pure joy of playing baseball.

The reader will find amusing stories of baseball from behind the scenes from the Singing Senators to the hot dog he once took to the mound. Using his own personal history and detailed accounts, he's able to weave the statistical giants of the game with amusing and hard-luck tales of a sport that was and still is "America's Pastime."

Johnny Pesky
Boston Red Sox

7

Introduction

On June 11, 1999, I was honored to be a part of a celebration at Shea Stadium honoring the 60th anniversary of Ted Williams' first appearance in the major leagues in 1939. The Mets were hosting the Boston Red Sox in the opening series of inter-league competition. In attendance were 45,000 fans! Special guests included Elden Auker, a pitcher on the 1939 Red Sox; Walt Dropo and Billy Klaus, teammates with Ted during the 1950s; Yogi Berra of the Yankees; Tommy Lasorda, Hall of Fame manager with the Dodgers; Rusty Staub and Tom Seaver of the 1969 championship Mets; and Jack Fisher of the Baltimore Orioles, who gave up Williams' 521st home run on his last official time at bat in his career.

All of us were invited to have breakfast with Williams at eight o'clock in his hotel suite. Ted was confined to a wheelchair, but it was soon apparent that his mental capacity and interest in baseball had not diminished in anyway. His knowledge and opinion of current players, teams, and tendencies in baseball were right on target, and his recall of games, players and incidents that took place years before was as vivid and alive as the day they took place. At noon, Ted's son, John Henry, reminded his dad that he had a television interview in a few minutes. "To hell with it!" Ted grumbled. "What could be better than this, being with old friends and teammates, and talking about the greatest game ever played."

As we left the suite and headed for the elevator, I remarked to Jean Klaus, Billy's wife, " I bet that was really boring for you ladies sitting for three hours listening to a bunch of old ballplayers telling stories?"

"No", she replied. "It was really great because when you guys are gone you'll take these great stories with you and they'll be lost forever."

Her statement and my realization that I wanted to leave an impression of my life in baseball with my children, grandchildren, future generations of family, close friends, and baseball fans who will enjoy these stories about the greats and not so greats, because they are flavored with the inside taste of baseball, prompted me to write this book.

I was skiny and all legs during my high school days.

The famous Forbes Field where I tried out for the Boston Red Sox.

Chapter 1

Being Recruited

When I was playing high school and semi-pro baseball, Cable "Socko" McCarey was the top scout for the Boston Red Sox in the Pittsburgh area. He had been watching me develop since my freshman year in high school. During my senior year, the competition for my services heightened among the teams that had shown an interest in me. Scouts from the Pittsburgh Pirates, Cincinnati Reds, Brooklyn Dodgers, New York Giants, and the Boston Red Sox also liked me. Furthermore, a number of colleges wanted me to play football, basketball, and baseball. I was voted All-City in three sports. I had scholarship offers from Michigan, Michigan State, UCLA, Penn State and Pitt. I guess you might say I had my share of options?

11

In late June of 1949, the Red Sox and Pirates were scheduled to play an exhibition game at Forbes Field in Pittsburgh. The Giants, Pirates, and Reds had me throw batting practice each time they came to Pittsburgh. Socko made arrangements for me to throw batting practice to show some of the Red Sox brass why he was so interested in signing me.

The visitor's clubhouse man at Forbes Field provided me with a Red Sox uniform, and before long I was warming up to throw batting practice. I didn't know it at the time, but big league baseball players do not like to hit against young prospects that may be wilder than a New Year's eve celebration in New York. I must say that the Red Sox hitters were great. They soon recognized that I was around the plate most of the time, so they relaxed a bit and so did I as I worked through the reserve players. Then I reached down for the rosin bag and when I looked up and turned toward home plate. Ted Williams was adjusting himself in the batter's box. He was my idol since I can remember. I must have read a million articles about him not swinging at a pitch if it were an inch off the plate. Now I'd find out. I was nervous, real nervous, and Ted knew it. "Hey, kid, just get it over the plate!" Williams yelled.

Did he say what I thought he said? He nodded his head and pointed his bat toward the mound. "You're doing a good job. Just lay it right down the middle. You'll be fine."

I went from wanting to crawl under the rubber to being nine feet tall on top of it. I laid each pitch right down the middle. Good speed. Good fastball. The kind of pitch a major league hitter will crush, which is exactly what Williams did, which is what batting practice is all about, which is what Williams did to most pitchers in a game anyway. To tell the truth, I didn't think he made any distinction between batting practice and hitting in a league game. If the balls were thrown in his direction, in the strike zone, he would rip at it. Hit it! Crack! Ted created the unmistakable sound that makes baseball unique in American sports.

Every pitch I threw to Williams caused me to think he wasn't thrilled with my pitching. He talked to himself, mumbled. Here I am pitching batting practice to Ted Williams, and I got him talking to himself. Talk about screwing up! Later I would find out that he always talked to himself during batting practice, for a definite purpose. Years later, I learned that Ted always had a purpose for everything he did. Batting practice was not just warming up for the game; it was hitting, and he took every swing

12

seriously. He was born to hit!

After batting practice, I went to the Red Sox locker room to take a shower. I was getting dressed when Ted came in. He came over to me. "Mr. Williams," I said, mainly because I didn't know what else to say. I was hardly going to say, "Hi, Ted!" As it was, I nearly choked. I was that nervous, but it didn't make much difference because I don't think he even heard what I called him, or that he much cared. He put his hand on my shoulder. I don't think I washed that shoulder it for a month or more.

"Good job, kid. You should sign with the Red Sox!"

"Ahh, ummm, ahhh," I mumbled. All that I could coax out of my larynx that suddenly was in spasm, frozen at full-choke.

Ted continued with his reasoning, "Some clubs have a million farm teams from the bush leagues to Triple-A. The Red Sox only have eight. You'll get to the majors faster with the Sox if you have the stuff, and I'd say from what you showed me tonight, you do."

I nodded. I believe that I would have signed with the Komoko Brown Bears, if Ted had suggested I do so. Little did I know at that time that my best performance in baseball would be in a Red Sox uniform.

After my experience throwing batting practice to the Red Sox at Forbes Field and speaking with Ted Williams, my heart belonged to Boston. However, the Giants continued to show a great interest in signing me. I threw batting practice again when they returned to Pittsburgh later that summer and my father, brother, and I met with the Giants head scout and manager Leo Durocher. They were offering a modest signing bonus of $500 and a Class C contract at $150 a month. We decided to wait and see what the Red Sox would offer. I had not graduated from high school yet, and I had not signed an agreement to attend a college. No agents existed at this time or the baseball draft. Signing a professional contract was up to the individual. Any professional team was permitted to approach any player who had completed high school. The search for the best player was a bidding war with the talent going to the highest bidder.

After school had let out for the summer, I was playing semi-pro baseball. One evening my coach told me the head scout for the Giants was there to see me pitch. I had pitched a complete game the night before, but being a kid, and not too smart, it never occurred to me that pitchers didn't pitch back-to-back games, so I agreed to pitch. I threw the whole game and we won, but I would say it was not one of my better outings. The

Giant's scout approached me after the game. He suggested I accept one of the college offers I'd received. I was stunned! In his opinion was I was too light, didn't throw hard enough, and most likely would not make it in pro baseball. I was sick, really sick. I don't think I ate or slept for the next week. It never occurred to me or anyone else, for that matter, to tell the Giant's scout that I had just pitched a full game the night before.

Finally, my family helped me make the decision to go to college. Perhaps college was the best thing for me. I could play all three sports. I accepted a full athletic scholarship to the University of Pittsburgh. Staying at home for college made it easier for my family to watch me play.

I no sooner enrolled at Pitt than the new football coach, who just happened to use the same system that I was accustomed to playing quarterback with in high school, called me into his office to talk about me playing football. Since freshmen were not permitted to play varsity sports, we reached an agreement for me to wait until the following year before joining the football program. I had already committed myself to playing basketball, and baseball. I also had a job that was part of the scholarship offer.

The basketball season turned out to be a real bummer for me. Pitt, under Dr. Carlson, a great basketball coach, used a system of picks, screens, and a rotation called the figure eight that permitted shooting the ball only if it were a lay-up. To give you an example and the results of how his system worked, Pitt had a varsity game that year with Penn State and the score was 3-2 at halftime. For a guy that led the city in scoring as a senior, this was a real handicap for me. It was a long basketball season, and I found myself looking forward to the sounds of spring — the baseball pounding into the catcher's mitt and the crack of the ball hitting the bat. After all, baseball was my first love.

Freshman baseball at Pitt left a great deal to be desired as well. College baseball in those days was still in its infancy. The College World Series began in 1947 and college players weren't given the attention from the pros like they are today. Freshman baseball was bad. I had been pitching against college players since I was fifteen, and I began to get the feeling that college baseball at Pitt would not prepare me for a professional career in baseball. I just prayed that the Giant's scout was wrong about my size and fastball, and that the Red Sox would still be interested in me.

Along about this time I began to realize that my parents weren't well

14

off. My father had worked forty-two years at Union Switch and Signal Company. They made switches for railroad crossings. I don't believe my dad went to work happy one day in his life, but he went everyday. He was a farmer at heart and he had decided to retire on a modest pension. My parents realized that a modest pension would not fulfill their needs in post-war America. I wanted to help them out.

Late in June, after the college season ended, Socko came to our home following a semi-pro baseball game. He offered me a signing bonus of $3,000 and a Class A contract at Scranton of the Eastern League. This was more than the Giants had offered me the previous year, but my brother Whitey had read the bonus baby stories, and was convinced that good prospects were receiving under-the-table money above the $6,000 baseball permitted. High school and college players that possessed superior ability in the eyes of the scouts were getting $50,000 to $100,000 for signing a baseball contract. Bonuses finally reached the point that the commissioner of baseball passed a rule stating that any player who received more than $6,000 to sign a contract would have to remain on the major league roster for two seasons before he could be optioned to the farm system. This would be a real albatross for those teams fighting for the pennant. I was delighted with the Red Sox offer because I knew that most kids started in Class D and worked their way up through the system.

My brother informed Socko that my parents wanted me to sign with Pittsburgh so they could see me play, and we had a meeting with the Pirates organization the next day. Actually he was stretching the truth just a little. McCarey was not about to lose me to Pittsburgh or anyone else. He simply reached down, picked up his briefcase and opened it upside down on the table. Outpoured more green cash than we had ever seen. Three thousand one-dollar bills to be exact! My parents were from Germany, and to them this must have looked like enough money to buy the world. My dad, a very religious man, mumbled something about not wanting me to play on Sunday, the Lord's Day, but he could not take his eyes from the money as he picked up the pen to sign. I decided to share the money with my parents. They took the cash and I took the check. The money helped them through some hard times and launched my baseball career.

Three years later, I was with the Red Sox when we broke from spring training and headed north to open the season. We flew to Arizona, to take on the Giants before going on to Boston to open the season. I pitched two perfect innings against the Giants that day. Following the game, the Giants scout, the same scout who told me I would not make it in the big leagues, approached me. "You've come a long way in a short period of time," he said. "Good luck." Oh, by the way, I finally told him about the back-to-back pitching assignments. He just smiled and replied, "That's life, ain't it?"

During my high school days, I also played for the Emory American Legion baseball team.

16

I'm at the front of this family photo.

Chapter 2
How It All Began

During the post-depression days, three organizations contributed to my interest in athletics: Kingsley House, our neighborhood version of the YMCA; the Emory Methodist Church softball team; and the summer recreation program run by the school district. My dad was the manager of the church team and my two brothers also played on the team. I traveled with them to every game and in the process picked up some impressive skills that would carry over to my future baseball career.

"Pop" Yetter ran the athletic programs at Kingsley House. His efforts gave me a deep interest in football and basketball. The athletic skills I learned during this period laid the foundation for my participation at Dillworth Elementary School and Peabody High School. During my four years at Peabody High School, the team traveled all over Pittsburgh to play schools in the City League. I was always amazed to look into the stands and find my father sitting there. One thought always entered my mind, "How did he get here?" My dad never missed a game during my high school career in any sport, whether it be baseball, football, basketball, or volleyball, or an American Legion baseball game during the summer.

My father influenced me by example. Fred or Dick, as his friends knew him — his first name was Frederick — was a true lover of God, the nature of the world about him, and his family. He was a small, quiet man, a solitary person, although not a bit unfriendly. He was extremely polite. I would often be waiting for him at the streetcar stop when he returned from work in the afternoon, and we would walk the two miles or so to our home. He would tip his hat to every women we passed regardless of their age or race. He was a gentleman to the utmost, proud of his German heritage and devoted to the land of the free and the home of the brave. He stood five feet tall and tipped the scales at a solid 101, about the size of a jockey. He never owned a car. He walked almost everywhere he went taking a streetcar or bus only when it was necessary to get where he was going.

Sunday was the Lord's Day in our home and after church the remainder of the day, following Sunday dinner, was family time. I was the last of five children two boys, Fred and Nevin, and two sisters, Katherine and Mary Lou. Eleven years separated my youngest sister and me. I assume my arrival on the scene was a bit of a surprise since dad was well into his late forties when I bounced into being. By the time I reached the seventh grade I was the only child at home.

World War II started and my dad, like most men in their fifties, was working 10 to 12 hours a day six days a week to help the war effort. As a result he never had the time, the know-how, or the athletic skills to enable him to play catch or kick a football with me. His age also prevented him from doing so.

One thing that I have pondered over for years is the fact my dad never commented on a game I took part in, not an utterance, a smile, a frown, a hint of any kind that would indicate his feelings or opinion in any way. Still, I had this deep feeling of love that shown in his eyes and from his every action. I knew that I was his reason to live! It was something I never questioned. I learned more from dad about life, people, faith, love, and

18

respect for women, my elders, and the value of truth and keeping your word, determination and hard work, principles I've tried to carry with me all my life.

My mother was just the opposite of my dad. He was five-foot tall and never weighed over 100 pounds in his life. She, on the other hand, was a big-big woman at least six foot tall with the strength to support a back-hand that quickly gained my respect at an early age. Her maiden name was Thersa Mae Skidmore. When I did something that did not please her, she let out with a verbal tongue-lashing, in German that would bring a blush to a sailor's face and a welt to a certain part of my anatomy. I stayed out of her reach as much as humanly possible. On her more gentle side, she had a heart of gold, never failing to reach out to anyone who had a need she could do something about. When her younger sister passed away and her husband left town, mom never hesitated to take in her only child, Alice, and raise her as her own. In fact, I always considered Alice as a sister because she was part of the family long before I came along, and she lived with us until she married.

Mom had a few characteristics that brought me concern. She had, for the most part, very little education. She didn't spell or write very well and when I missed school she'd write me a note that was so badly spelled and structured that often I was unable to read what she had written. This embarrassed me and I carried it with me most of my life. She also had a physical impairment known as "hammer toes." Her feet were so badly deformed that she could hardly walk at times. She would seek relief by wearing old, comfortable shoes, often my tennis shoes and cut holes in the toe area to allow her feet to gain relief from the pressing pain caused by the shoe.

Her feet resulted in the "Herb Fishman incident." Herbie was a talented guard on the high school basketball team. One day I forgot my gym shoes and rather that lose grade points in gym class, I borrowed Herb's shoes. The problem is I took them home with me and didn't return them for several weeks. By then basketball practice had begun and Herb came looking for his shoes. I explained that they were at home, which was just a block from the school, and told him ask my mother for the shoes and she would give them to him. Later that day, Herb came to practice without the shoes, but laughing so hard it was almost impossible for him to stop laughing long enough to relate the story of him knocking on the door and

I played quarterback on the football team.

asking my mom for his tennis shoes. He happened to look down at my mother's feet and lo and behold she had his tennis shoes on with the holes cut in the tops and her toes sticking out like peanut growing up through the soil. Herb let out a horrified scream that frightened my mother, which set her off muttering a string of German words that in turn caused Herb to throw up his hands in despair as she tried to take off the shoes and give them to him. As you might expect this incident was a topic of conversation until long after graduation. I might add it was brought to my attention again nearly forty years later at a class reunion. Needless to say, my mom's feet were most embarrasing to me.

I never wanted my mother to attend any of my games, especially football, because whenever I was tackled or knocked down she would let out a howl of grief that arose above the voice of the crowd, the cheers of the cheerleaders, and the sounds from the field. She'd yell, "Don't hurt my baby!" I wanted to hide.

When she passed away at age 83, people came from all over the city and related to me wonderful heartwarming stories of her kindness, consideration, and outright love she poured out on her friends and neighbors. I guess when I see her again I'm going to find it necessary to apologize to her.

Another person who influenced my development in baseball was my high school coach. I first met him when I was attending Dilworth Elementary School. I'd walk about a mile and a half to school everyday. No school buses in those days. My daily walk to and from school carried me past the athletic field at Peabody High School. In the fall, I would stop and watch football practice through the 20-foot high chain-link fence that enclosed the east side of the athletic field. Sometimes I got brave and walked through the gate and onto the field so I could hear what the coach was saying. One day, at the conclusion of practice he said, "Hi."

I responded, "My name is Russ Kemmerer and when I come to Peabody, I'm going to play football for you."

"Good, I'll look for you," he answered.

That was my introduction to coach Richard S. Meyers, the man who perhaps determined the direction my life would take more than anyone else. Perhaps I was drawn to him because in many ways he resembled my father, but a little larger at perhaps five-foot-five inches and 150 pounds. He was also German and wore one of those little brush mustaches like Adolph Hitler. However, the resemblence stopped there. I wasn't the only one he influenced. I can name at least ten from my graduating high school class that went into education and coaching because of his significance, and I am certain there is a long, long list of others who traveled the same course for the same reason.

The public schools in Pittsburgh graduated classes in January as well as June. I happened to be in the group of January graduates from my elementary school. The first day I walked into the hallowed halls of Peabody, I was right smack-dab in the middle of the basketball season. The very first thing I did was to go to coach Meyers office before school started and asked if I could come out for basketball. He never made any excuses about it being the middle of the season or too late this year or hesitated in any other way. He replied, "We begin practice about 30 minutes after school, bring your gym shoes and we'll give you a practice uniform." Thus, I began my high school athletic career and begin to take in the lasting influence this man would have on the direction my life would take.

For the next four years, I played football and basketball for coach Meyers. I would describe his approach to coaching and teaching as gentle toughness. He explained the plays and what he wanted done. He never cussed or went off on a screaming tangent, but he wasn't opposed to grabbing a jersey or laying a foot on a backside when necessary. His strongest expression was "Judas Priest," a term used by every man who ever played for him. Meyers wanted his players to know and understand his system and the game of football. He insisted that his quarterback know every play and what every position did on every play. He seldom sent in instructions from the sidelines. He was truly a coach far ahead of his time.

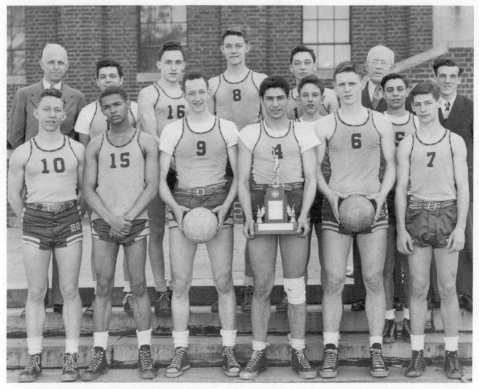

I wore #9 on the volleyball team.

I used his system for years at every level of football, from junior league to college, and always found it effective. Many of the things he taught did not show up in the college game for many years. Football in those days was just coming out of the single wing era and into the winged-T stage, and Meyers was an inventive, imaginative coach.

I played halfback my freshman year, but came to the conclusion early in the season that it might not be my position. That opinion was emphasized by a defensive end from Turtle Creek High School by the name of Leon Hart, who flattened me the first time I ran off tackle. In case the name doesn't ring a bell, Hart was an All-American at Notre Dame and Pro Football Hall of Fame end with the Detroit Lions. By the end of the season I settled comfortably into the quarterback position behind senior, Paul Palumbo. I played that position the remainder of my high school career and was offered several scholarships at major universities.

Coach Meyers' basketball teams were always at the top of the standings. His coaching was genius. We managed to win the city championship my sophomore year. We went onto win two more Section I titles as well as one regional trophy. However, it was the man far more than the coach that drew men to follow him into the teaching and coaching profession. Those who played for him in the 1940s and 1950s still meet once a month for lunch. This ritual has continued now for more than fifty years. Many former players are responsible for the Peabody Old Crocks Old Jocks organization, but I believe that the underlying reason we continue to meet is the bond that united us through coach Meyers. When he passed on a few years ago, former players and wives came from all over the country to pay their last respects. He was loved and remembered by everyone he touched.

Then there was Denny Moore, no relation to the Irish stew people. He was a claims adjuster for the Yellow Cab Company in Pittsburgh, but baseball was his thing. He had a little minor league experience, one older son who was playing in the minor leagues at the AA level and a younger son Joe, who played on our team. Denny had an inspired love for baseball. He came along when I was trying to break into a tough semi-pro league that had many of the top prospects in the area. One of his friends was

I'm sitting (second from the right) in this photo of our basketball team.

Donie Bush, the head scout for the Pittsburgh Pirates. I was a skinny fifteen-year-old kid with natural raw talent, but Bush knew I would be overmatched in this league. He recommended to Moore that he take me for his team so that I could get the necessary experience to move up the baseball ladder. It was one of the best things that ever happened to me. I learned more about baseball from Denny than I imagined possible. Every day he would pick up as many of us kids as he could find during his lunch hour and take us to a field or any vacant lot and work with us on hitting, fielding and pitching. Some days we spent the whole time working on a single thing, like a pick-off play or a pitcher's move to first base. By the time I was ready to move to Bush's team the following year, I gained more baseball knowledge than I ever dreamed possible. This knowledge that proved helpful when I went into pro ball.

Several players on the team went onto play in the major leagues, such as Bob and Eddie Sadowski. Bob pitched for the Cardinals, Phillies, White Sox, and Angels. Eddie caught with the Red Sox, Angels, and Braves. Frank Thomas had a great career with the Pirates and several other teams. Bob Purkey threw for the Pirates, Reds, and Cardinals. George Susce pitched with Boston and Detroit. Moore had his hand in the making of many successful baseball players. He loved the game and was committed to help and teach baseball. I have never forgotten what he did for me! I plan to continue to do the same for boys today.

After I nearly pitched a no-hitter in Louisville, I joined my supporting cast of home run hitters: (left to right) Roy Buckwalter, Harry Agganis and Charlie Maxwell.

Chapter 3
Playing in the Minors

The third week of June in 1951 I completed my second semester at Pitt and made signing arrangements with the Red Sox. The Scranton Red Sox of the Class-A Eastern League was fighting for the league title. I figured it would be difficult to work me into the rotation at this point in the season and hinder their chances of winning a championship. Most minor league teams finish their seasons the first week in September, so the decision was made to permit me to remain in Pittsburgh and finish out the season with Dormont of the Greater Pittsburgh League. The league was the cream of semi-pro baseball in the area. Many players had a year or more of minor league experience, but for one reason or another, decided to give up pro baseball. The reputation of the league was

25

so highly regarded it was not a major decision for Boston to allow me to finish the 1950 season at home in Pittsburgh. After the season ended, I got married to a girl named Betty Hasley, who I grew up with.

I spent a great deal of time that summer watching and talking to players in the league, who had a taste of pro ball. They were by far the best talent in the league. I had a recurring thought, "If these guys couldn't make the grade in Class C or D, how much better were the guys that did?" The stories told about conditions and travel put me on edge, and I began to wonder if perhaps I too would be back in the Greater Pittsburgh League in a year or so. The tales indicated that the pay was low, the food terrible, travel tiring, and conditions impossible. I began to have doubts about my success in pro baseball. These guys played at the lowest levels of professional baseball, Class D, and failed to make the cut after spring training. I had signed a Class A contract, three levels higher. How much tougher would that be for a raw rookie fresh out of high school?

Early in February, I found myself sitting on an airplane headed for Ocala, Florida. I had been assigned to spring training with Birmingham of the AA Southern League. If I had doubt, about the caliber of A baseball, what would AA be like? Adding to this pressure were three facts. First, I was on my very first plane ride Secondly, this was my first-ever journey away from home, with the exception of church camp where I got so homesick and couldn't hit or catch a ball to save my soul. In fact, I was by far the worst player in the church camp. Third, I didn't know a single player in training camp. It was my first night in a hotel, something I would grow accustomed to in the next 15 years. To top it off, my roommate was a good "ole" Southern boy from Gaffney, South Carolina, and for the life of me I could not understand what "Y'all" meant, what grits were, and why would anyone want to put tobacco, better known as a chaw, into his mouth? His name was Alfeus, "Al" for short, Curtis and we are still friends today.

At breakfast that first day I got my first taste of southern grits and thick-sliced bacon. Following breakfast we reported to the baseball field for my first day of spring training. I had thoughts of church camp. I prayed I would be able to throw and hit the ball better than I had done there, but before we reached the end of the first week, I knew I had nothing to fear. I threw faster than most, and my curveball was the talk of training camp. About the third day, Johnny Murphy, the head of the Red Sox minor league operation, called me to the batting cage. "Socko told me you're a pretty good hitter so pick a bat from the rack, get into the cage, and take a few cuts."

I was facing a big left-handed kid from Alabama, Paul Perry, and I never came close to his first three pitches. Wow, he was fast! I believe I touched his fourth pitch. Johnny Murphy gave me some words of advice, "Relax and keep your eyes on the ball. You'll be fine."

I lined the next pitch between third and short. I then stroked a soft shot into right center. I began to feel pretty good. Murphy called to the pitcher, "Paul, let's see what he can do with your breaking ball." He threw a high, hanging curve, my favorite pitch, and I drilled it over the left field fence. "Not bad, not bad, Socko gave us the right dope about you, go back out and shag balls." That day all my fears passed I knew I could play with these guys.

Spring training flew by. I was in love; in love with every minute I was on the field. I worked harder than I had ever worked in my life, and I loved every minute of it. I could hardly wait for practice each day.

Friendships blossomed. I got to know Al Curtis, Gene Stephens, Ike Delock, Al Schroll, Tommy Umphlete, Charlie Maxwell, Sammy White, Faye Throneberry, Neil Chrisley, Frank Malzone, and Hershel Freeman. These were guys in camp who went on to play in the majors.

In review of my first spring training, I gained confidence I could compete, learned to love grits, took my first chaw, was introduced to Southern cooking, smoked my first Cuban cigar, and made life- long friendships. It was one of the happiest times of my life. I was being paid for doing what I had done just for fun and what I loved doing more than anything in the world. When spring training ended, White, Freeman, Delock, and Malzone remained with the Birmingham Barons. I was sent to Roanoke of the Class B Piedmont League.

My first spring training in professional baseball raised my confidence sky high. I looked forward to my first pro season with great anticipation. Roanoke, Virginia, is a beautiful city and a fantastic place to begin a career. The first few days in town were spent on the ball diamond, looking for a place to live, and just checking everything out in the stores, places to eat, shop and more importantly, the girls. I found a nice room with an elderly couple. The home sat high on a hill, overlooking the city about a mile from the ballpark, just a nice walk to and from the field each day.

For some reason, I missed the bellowing of the steel mills, the smell of Iron City Beer, and the coal smell that hung over Pittsburgh and drifted with the evening breeze from one side of the city to the other. What is it they say: "You can take the boy out of the city, but you can't take the city out of the boy."

I soon learned that the Piedmont League was a far cry from the Greater Pittsburgh League. The players were bigger, stronger, more experienced, and better athletes than any I had played against. For the first time in my life I experienced a right-handed hitter belting my best curve ball over the right field fence. It may have been the first time but it most certainly was not the last. By the way, that hitter was Moose Skowron, who went on to have a great career with the Yankees. I would face him for the remainder of my career.

I did fine in the spring when the weather remained cool, but as May moved into June the humidity began to take effect on my stamina. My starts fluctuated, one good game followed by a bad one. My problem seemed to be endurance; I was running out of gas around the sixth inning. I struggled.

Our manager was a fireball, former major league catcher, Walter Millies, who had played briefly for the Chicago Cubs. Walt was a no-nonsense disciplinarian who demanded one-hundred-ten-percent effort, one hundred percent of the time. We nicknamed him, "The Rattler." He possessed the ability to strike out, with stinging remarks, at the least expected times. One afternoon, following one of my poor outings, he called me into his office. "You're not getting beat by the other teams, you're getting beat by something you can't control, the heat. Why in the hell would you let the heat bother you? Your butt must be out of shape! From now on you will run twenty minutes each, morning every day, when we're at home, except when your starting."

Needless to say, Mr. Millies was not one of my favorite people. Every time I turned around he was "hissing" at me like a rattlesnake coiled to strike for one little thing or another. I stayed as far from him as possible. About a week before the season ended in September, Walt called me into his office. I prepared for his coil and strike. Much to my surprise, he greeted me with a smile and a handshake. He congratulated me on a good season and informed me that I was going to report to Boston for the remainder of the year. I was not officially joining the club; however, they wanted to work with me. I would throw batting practice and work out with the team.

When I arrived in Boston, Murphy greeted me in his office. The first words he spoke to me echoed around in my head, when he said, "Walt Millies really liked you."

"Are you kidding? He hated me!" I replied.

"Come with me," he said, and proceeded to usher me into the scouting room. Each manager in the farm system had to send a weekly report on each player on his team, and a monthly report on each player in the league. He began to read parts of Walt's reports. "Best pitching prospect in the league." "Most improved pitcher." "Can't miss ability, great attitude," and on and on. I could hardly believe my ears. I was speechless!

Millies had predicted Skowron and I would have long, successful major league careers. One of the mistakes we so often make when we're young is to jump to misunderstood conclusions because we are incapable of looking at the situation from any perspective but our own. Walt realized that my athletic ability was at a level that allowed me to reach goals without extra effort. He also knew that playing in the major leagues would require an effort beyond that which I had ever experienced. He was determined to see that I would not miss my opportunity because of an easygoing attitude. He understood that I was the type of athlete that coaches seldom had to discipline. He was also certain that his hard-nosed approach would drive me to an I'll-show-you attitude. He was right. The lesson I learned was not to judge a person too quickly.

Later in my career when I was with the White Sox, I met Millies and his family. They were living in Chicago. We exchanged cards and letters, and remained friends until his death. One other thing, I took his advice about not allowing things you can't control to bother you. The advice he gave me about the weather prolonged my career. I learned to ignore the heat instead of feeling the heat. I used it to my advantage and thus gained the reputation of loving to pitch in extremely hot weather. This and the fact that I could pitch every day was the reason why later in my career the White Sox traded for me in 1962. When the Houston was organized, the Colts wanted me for the same reason — I could take the heat!

All the fears I had going into the season regarding my ability to play professional baseball dissipated one by one in the minors. I loved the bus travel. We played cards, looked at the girls, took in movies, sang, played outlandish pranks on each other, and spent time on the beach. We won, lost, were rained out, and got paid for playing baseball. I never imagined that it was possible to be paid for doing what you really loved. It was, without doubt, the best time of my life! God had blessed me with athletic talent and now I was paid for using that talent.

After the season ended, I had something else to look forward to, which was being a father. My first son, Rusty, was born in November.

My second professional season began early and with an unexpected surprise. The Red Sox made a decision to bring all of the top minor league prospects in their system to Sarasota, Florida, for a special training session in early January 1952. There were two reasons for this decision. First, many of the team's star players were reaching the end of their careers, such as Dom DiMaggio, Vern Stephens, Bobby Doerr, and Johnny Pesky. Secondly, the team had replaced Steve O'Neill with Lou Boudreau as their new manager. The early training sessions gave Boudreau the chance to see Boston's top minor league prospects and evaluate them personally, and it gave him a good idea of the veterans that he could trade for younger talent.

We reported to camp the first week in January. Many of the players were the same ones I was at spring training with the previous year. This time around there was no homesick feeling; it was just a matter of renewing old acquaintances. The coaching staff worked us hard every day, seven days a week. It was a learning process in a very competitive atmosphere. We went through drill after drill on the fundamentals of baseball: covering first base, fielding bunts, recognizing the proper base to throw to, leading the second baseman or shortstop as he moved to make the double play, hitting the cutoff man with the throw from the outfield, and last but not least for pitchers, backing up the bases for possible overthrows. We threw batting practice every other day, and even got to take a turn in the batting cage; pitchers went to bat in those days. We took our swings and laid down enough bunts to do it in our sleep.

The final two weeks or so of camp we broke up into teams and played inter-squad games. That special spring training was another great and wonderful experience. We had quite a bit of free time in the afternoons and evenings. We spent this time fishing, going to the movies, checking out the town, looking over the ladies, and hanging around the hotel. We did not receive a paycheck during this time, but all expenses were covered and we signed at the hotel for three meals a day. The only comment I could possibly make was, "How can it be any better than this?"

This special camp lasted about a month then it was time for the pitchers and catchers on the major league roster to report for spring training. The date was February 15, 1952, and it was the day that many of us received the second surprise of the spring. About a dozen of us were told that we would remain with the club during spring training, including me. Many of the veteran players came into camp early with the pitchers. The fact that the younger pitchers were in shape made it possible for the players on the roster to get in a lot of batting practice before they actually had to report on March 1. Players like George Kell, Walt Dropo, Billy Goodman, Stephens, Don Lenhardt, and Clyde Vollmer took advantage of this opportunity.

Spring training in those days was quite a bit different than what players experience today. In my era, most players had a job during the off-season. For example, Robin Roberts worked in a box factory. Yogi Berra and Phil Rizzuto worked in a clothing store. I worked in a steel mill. Our contracts actually prohibited and discouraged us from lifting weights or taking part in contact sports such as basketball, football, or hockey. Seldom did any of us that lived in the cold country try to throw prior to spring training. In fact any activity that required the use of muscles used in baseball was taboo. Swimming, weight lifting, or golf was prohibited. In short, the purpose of spring training was to get in shape. This opened the door for many of the young players, like myself, to show our talents. We actually played in the early spring games, while the veterans got themselves into shape.

Several of us with Class A contracts were sent to the Louisville Colonels, Triple-A training camp in Deland, Florida. When the Colonels broke training camp, I was still on the team, and prior to the start of the American Association season I signed a Louisville contract for a sizable increase. This was quite a jump from Class B at Roanoke to Triple-A in Louisville.

Most noticeable was the experience of the players. Each team was stacked with former major league players who were either finishing out their careers, or hoping for one last shot at a big league job. At the other end of the line were the prospects, those players like myself, who were considered future big leaguers. We were being prepared to move on to

Boston as soon as we had the necessary experience. The average age of a rookie pitcher making the major league team in those days was about twenty- five. The feeling was you needed that kind of experience before you would even be given a shot at making the big time. This philosophy changed a few years later when teams began to take a chance on 21-year-old pitchers.

Another big change in the league was the method of travel. All minor league teams from Class D to AA, traveled by bus. Triple-A teams went by train, with a private sleeping car for the players. This was necessary because the cities were a greater distance from each other than those in the lower leagues. The city or private investors, who had an affiliation with a major league franchise, owned most teams at this level of baseball. Teams in those days stayed fairly stable in regard to veteran players. Usually it was the prospects that were moved up or down so they can play regularly.

My first season at Louisville was a learning experience, to say the least. The veteran players in the league soon learned to read young pitchers, laying back and waiting on the fastball when they were ahead in the count. Young pitchers usually rely on their best pitch when they are behind in the count. Most often the best pitch is a fastball, and experienced hitters jump on fastballs. Learning to throw a pitch other than a fastball when you are behind in the count is perhaps the most important lesson to learn. Your survival in higher baseball depends on the development of a change up, changing speeds on the fastball, and being able to throw a breaking ball when behind in the count. Without these tools, there is little chance of a long major league career.

The 1953 season began with an invitation to go to spring training with the Red Sox. I was determined to show the Red Sox management that I had accepted and conquered the challenges they had placed before me at the end of the 1952 season. I also met Bob Friend. He had suffered through a season with the Pirates with a team that only won 42 games while losing 112. We were both determined to improve both our personal records and our team records. We worked out five days a week at the local YMCA. Not a day went by that we didn't discuss pitching techniques and strategies. When it came time to report to spring training, we were both in the greatest physical and mental shape of our lives.

The hard work paid off. I pitched extremely well in a number of exhibition games, so well in fact, that when the team broke training camp I was still on the roster for the trip back to Boston. The day before the season opened, Boudreau called me into his office and explained that he had planned on keeping me with the team. I was not, however, on the official twenty-five man team roster. They only had one spot open, and due to an injury they needed to sign an outfielder. As a result I was being optioned to Louisville. Actually, I was given a new contract with a nice raise. Boudreau challenged me to have a great season with the Colonels so that I would be called up when an opening occurred.

I was disappointed, very disappointed! At the same time, I knew that it was just a matter of time until I made the majors. I was determined to have a great year in Louisville and be headed back to the big leagues as quickly as possible. I believe I pitched with a vengeance. I felt that everyone who got a hit off me was actually stealing from me and at the same time keeping me from my goal of reaching the majors. The early part of the season, I ran into a series of bad luck outings. I lost several low scoring games, 1-0 and 2-1. It was almost as if I had to pitch a shutout and hit a home run to win. That fate haunted me my entire career. I ended up pitching in 34 games, winning eleven and losing eight. I threw nine complete games, pitched 188 innings, 109 strikeouts, and my earned run average was 3.40. I pitched two one-hitters. I came within an eyelash of one in St. Paul. We were playing the Saints and I had pitched a flawless game up until the last out in the bottom of the ninth. We were up 5-0, so I wasn't afraid of losing, but I was afraid of losing the no-hitter. An infield hit did me in and I missed the no-hiiter. I got the one-hitter, but it wasn't much of a consolation. With a little more support and luck, I might have easily won 18 games that season.

I loved playing in Louisville. The Colonels were a fun team. I had more fun and made more life-long friends than at anytime in my life. The combination of veterans and prospects made for strange bedfellows. Red Marion was our manager. We just about drove him out of baseball and his mind. Once when we traveled to St. Paul from Louisville, there was a long delay in Chicago because we had to wait on our connecting train to hitch us up. This gave us plenty of time to visit some of the local pubs. This, of course, resulted in some happy, playful ball players. Bob Smith, another pitcher, and I entered our sleeping car and were belted with pillows. This seemed like great fun so we laid in wait for the next unsuspecting sole to enter the car. Before too long, we had one of the best pillow fights you ever thought of being a part of going on. Feathers a foot deep covered the floor. We finally tired of it and settled into our bunks.

I remember awaking in the morning to the startled cries of the porter, "Lardy, lardy, Mr. Manager!" Marion finally entered the car with obscenities pouring forth from him along with shouts, grumbles, and threats. When he questioned us about it later, no one seemed to remember anything like that happening.

Years later I crossed paths with Red and we discussed that team. He said with a smile, "Without doubt, that was the strangest team I had ever been around in my career." Don't get me wrong, it was not that we played so badly; in fact, we were pretty good. It was simply our chemical make-up.

We had an outfielder, Bob Dipettro, who was not a bad ball gamer to say the least. Dipettro had a couple of shots with Boston but couldn't hold the position. This guy had talent! He could sing with Caruso, and he was a really funny guy with professional stand-up talent. When we were on the road we would find a dinner-club with a live band and good food to frequent after a game. Sooner or later, we would entice Bob to sing and entertain. Often the owner would close the doors and Bob would do his thing long after hours. This happened in more than one town, and before long, the owners were checking the schedule for our return, actually Bob's return.

On the last day of the season, Diprettro would go into his Babe Ruth act his last time at bat. He had a stocky built along the lines of Ruth, about 5-10"and 200 pounds. He would stuff a towel into his shirt, pull his pants up to his knees, go up to the plate left handed, although he batted right handed, point to the centerfield wall, and wait for the pitcher to throw a pitch. The veteran pitchers knew what was happening and would lay the pitch in there about half speed. At times, however, there would be a young pitcher, brought up from the lower minors, who didn't know this was a show; he would fire the ball toward the plate. "D," as we sometimes called him, would swing the bat. It didn't matter where he hit the ball or if he hit the ball, he would go into his Babe Ruth home run trot and circle the bases. The fans loved it, the teams loved it, and it was good for baseball.

Strange incidents happened all the time like nailing a guy's dress shoes to the locker floor as we rushed to get to the train station before the train pulled out without the team. Guys were running to catch the train in their stocking feet. Poor Red, no one ever knew anything about these incidents and no one ever said a thing about them.

Another strange event revolved around a pitcher who had pitched a no-hitter going into the bottom of the ninth inning. He managed to walk the first three hitters in the inning and that necessitated a visit to the mound by Marion. After some discussion, which became heated, Red decided to bring in a relief pitcher. The only problem was the starting pitcher wouldn't leave the mound or give the relief pitcher the ball. Finally, the umpire put another ball in play, causing the starting pitcher to throw the original baseball into the stands. The relief pitcher took his warm-up tosses and delivered his first pitch to the next hitter. It was soundly slammed into centerfield, scoring two runs and giving the home team the victory. Late that night, at the hotel, there were rumors of someone standing in the window, six stories up, urinating and howling obscenities directed at someone named Red.

We traveled by train and the most popular luggage for baseball players to carry were these footlocker type suitcases, made of masonite in St. Louis by the Hoffmeyer Company. On our return trip to Louisville, these were stacked on the platform outside of the railroad car. They were not the most difficult trunks to open, and players reported finding strange articles in their luggage when they unpacked, articles that would not normally be found there, such as delicate pieces of feminine clothing. Players had difficulty explaining to their wives just how these articles happened to appear among the dirty clothes. We were an outstanding baseball team who never quite reached its potential, but we sure had fun.

The Boston Red Sox sent out this photo postcard of me.

My Topps rookie card.

Chapter 4

Reaching the Goal

The 1954 season appeared it could be a transitional year for the Red Sox. Ted Williams had been discharged from the Marines late in the 1953 season. He returned to play in 37 games, batting 91 times, with 37 hits, 13 home runs, and a batting average of .407. That convinced the Red Sox management to sell or trade off several veterans picked up to fill the gap during his absence. They sold or traded George Kell, Dick Gernert, Hoot Evers, Floyd Baker, Del Wilber, and Tommy Umphlett, and replaced them with Harry Agganis, Grady Hatton, Jackie Jensen, Frank Sullivan, Tom Brewer, and Leo Kiley. Boston won 84 games in 1953 and it appeared, on paper, that these changes would enable them to contend with the Yankees for the American League pennant.

Spring training in 1954 began with high expectations; a sense of excitement prevailed around spring training. Williams' return and the changes in personnel gave a new look to the club. However, destiny often steps in to alter a team's course as it did one morning during batting practice. Williams had just taken his turn in the batting cage then pranced out to his position in left field to shag a few balls. A low line drive was hit in his direction. He attempted a shoestring catch. Suddenly, he tripped and lunged forward falling on his shoulder as he hit the ground. Pop! "I think I broke my collarbone!" he exclaimed. He slowly raised himself from the turf and headed for the clubhouse. Trainer Jack Fadden confirmed the break. The injury changed the direction the Red Sox would take, and stalled, at least for the time being, the drive to the top of the standings.

The injury to Williams also put a damper on the enthusiasm. The break was severe and would require surgery and pins to keep it stationary. He would be out four to six weeks of the season. The Red Sox had the choice of finding a veteran to fill the spot in left field or look to an untried rookie. Ted's injury hung over the team like a dark cloud and was the first of several incidents that occurred during the season that left a bad taste in the mouth of players and management alike.

When spring training ended the team had major questions to settle. Who would take Williams' spot in the outfield? Karl Olson and Faye Throneberry returned from the service and looked good at times during the spring. Gene Stephens had stepped in when Ted was in the service, so he was a possibility in the outfield. Stephens was a tall, thin, left-handed hitter out of Arkansas. In some ways he was a Williams look-a-like, and he had some talent. He had played in 21 games with Boston in 1952, and 87 games in 1953.

The pitching staff was also in question. Mel Parnell, Ellis Kinder, and Willard Nixon were the foundation of the staff, but there were a number of pitchers who had shown promise: Ike Delock, Brewer, Bill Henry, Leo Kiley, Al Curtis, Truman Clevenger, Dick Brodowski, and me. A decision needed to be reached on many of these young players.

I had a great spring training and talk was that I had cemented a starting assignment. We were traveling north with the Philadelphia Phillies, stopping en route at various cities as we made our way through North Carolina, Louisville, and onto Boston. In the game at Charlotte, things got a little heated. Carl Olson hit a home run for Boston and Karl Drews, the

Phil's pitcher, nailed the next hitter, Sammy White. I was warming up to go into the game, and as I came into the dugout manager Lou Boudreau had some special instructions for me. "That son-of-a-bitch Drews is first up. You drill him! Don't knock him down — drill him!"

Well, when the manager gives you instructions, you better follow them to the letter. Drews wore number 22. I took the knockdown sign from White, and fired my best fastball right at Karl's ribs. He turned his back away from the pitch to avoid being hit, however; the pitch struck him solidly right between the twos. Drew's teammates rushed the mound and the Sox came to protect me, which I found comforting since having 25 angry men charging the mound places one in jeopardy. Level heads prevailed and both clubs returned to the dugouts. When the side was retired and I returned to the dugout, Boudreau had a speech for the team, "Any SOB that can go out there and drill a man when he's told to has a place on this ball club," he shouted. Boudreau was impressed.

Protecting a teammate when the opposing team picks on him is a concept as old as baseball itself. A pitcher who fails to retaliate on behalf of a team member will lose him the respect of the team, while protecting them will gain him much creditability. When owners or managers make pointed, positive statements about players that relate to their team status, they are taken as Gospel. When they are not, the team's morale is placed in jeopardy. It is much like breaking a promise to a child, who can't tell the difference between a broken promise and a lie.

The day before the opening game of the season, I was called into Boudreau's office. He told me that I was being sent to Louisville. Being optioned to the minor leagues did not set well with me. Even the best managers don't make statements they can't back up. In all fairness to Boudreau, I believe his intent was to keep me. But fate moved its ugly head and decisions had to be made quickly. The reality of the situation needed to be addressed. The major concern of the Red Sox was to add hitting and outfield strength to make up for Williams' loss. The report on his healing was not positive. Many of the young players I mentioned had used up all of their options. Players with major league contracts could be optioned to the minor leagues three times, after that they had to be sold, traded, or released. I had only used two options. Thus, I won the prize. Back to Louisville!

Once again I set myself with determination and dug in with the attitude that I'd make the best of the situation because I could not control it, a lesson I learned back in Roanoke from Walt Millies. I pitched really well for the Colonels, but once again lack of run production kept my number of wins down. Herb Score was leading the American Association in wins, followed closely by Ike Delock of the Colonels. So, I was really surprised when manager Mike Higgins called me into his office in late May to tell me I was being called up to Boston. Of course I was overjoyed, but in all fairness, Delock had the most victories and was pitching great ball for Louisville. "Hell, you're leading the league in ERA, and with a few runs you would have won six or seven more games," Higgins explained. "Go to Boston and have a great year." I have always felt that the decision to call me up at this time had more to do with Boudreau's statement at spring training than it did with calling up the most deserving pitcher.

My wife and I gathered up our belongings, threw them in the trunk, put our son Rusty in the back seat, and headed for Pittsburgh. I was to join the team in Chicago, so it was necessary to leave Betty and Rusty in Pittsburgh with her mom and dad. When the team returned to Boston, I would find a home to rent and have them join me for the remainder of the season.

I didn't have to wait long before I appeared in my first major league game. The day after I arrived in Chicago, we were playing in a double-header. In the first game, the White Sox were up by five runs when I nervously came into the game. Minnie Minoso, who had doubled, was on second base with no outs. Catcher Sammy White came out to the mound and passed along a little information. "Russ, that's Minoso at second," he explained. "You've got to keep him close because he'll steal third in a flash, so keep your eyes on him."

I nodded and grumbled a "Yes," because the lump in my throat

Minnie Minoso

wouldn't allow me to speak. I took my warm up throws and looked out at Minnie as I fingered the rosin bag. I delivered my first pitch to Jim Rivera who was at the plate. Minnie had a fair lead, but didn't break for third. The pitch was a ball to Rivera. I thought to myself, I got to get the ball over the plate and watch Minoso at the same time. I took a deep breath, picked up the sign from Sammy, checked Minnie, turned toward home then suddenly turned and made a quick throw to second. It caught Minnie a little by surprise but he made it back to second easily. At least he knew I was watching him. Rivera fouled off the next pitch. The umpire threw me a new baseball so I went to the rear of the mound to pick up the rosin bag, but I made a mistake. Instead of rubbing up the ball while looking at Minoso, I looked at home plate. When I bent over to pick up the rosin bag Minnie took off for third. I never saw him and he made it without me offering a throw. Talk about feeling stupid, I certainly did. I got out of the inning and walked off the mound, with 55,000 fans applauding Minnie's base running and laughing at this green rookie at the same time.

A few innings later Minoso walked to lead off the inning. I had a pretty good move to first for a right-hander, so I gave him my three-quarter move to set him up. Sure enough he took one step too many, and I gave him my number one move. All his weight was committed to his right leg and he was late sliding back into first and was out. As he ran by me to the third base dugout he said, "We even." I said to myself well, "At least for now."

Sunday, July 18, 1954, started like any other Sunday for a rookie pitcher in his first big-league season with one exception: my three-year-old son Rusty had a bad case of the German measles. My wife Betty and I spent most of the night watching him, trying to keep his fever down. The Red Sox were scheduled to play Baltimore in a double-header that afternoon. The team followed a standard practice prior to a home game. Players reported to the ballpark four hours prior to a game. Pitchers, with the exception of the day's starter, took a short batting practice. The utility players were next in line to take hitting, followed by the day's starting lineup. The visiting team then took the field for batting practice. Infield practice for both teams was next on the agenda and then the event of the day — the game! It was mandatory for every rookie pitcher to be dressed and on the field when practice started. That was our responsibility. I was never late for batting practice!

Since Betty and I were renting a home in Needham, about a half hour's drive from Fenway Park, we decided it best to leave the car with her, just in case an emergency arose with Rusty. I made arrangements to ride to the ballpark with Frank Sullivan, a pitcher who lived across the street. I threw together a quick breakfast and waited for Frank to pick me up. I kissed Betty good-bye and told her to call Frank's wife if she needed anything. We made one stop to pick up Jackie Jensen, our right fielder, then drove to the ballpark. To be truthful, I felt as if I was deserting my wife and sick child at a time when they needed. But that was part of being a big-league ballplayer. People who have a normal job could call in sick — professional athletes don't have that option. It's just a part of life, period. If the truth were known, Betty was better off with me out of the house. This way she didn't have to take care of two of us — one sick with the measles and the other standing around fretting about the one sick with the measles.

Another part of being a big-league player is what happened when I got to Fenway. I had no sooner entered the clubhouse when Johnny Orlando, our clubhouse man, informed me that the manager wanted to see me in his office. My heart sank to the bottom of my stomach. Big league managers seldom call rookie pitchers to their office and when they do, it's generally not good news.

During the short time I had been with the team, I had pitched sparingly, mostly in games that were a lost cause. I could think of one reason, and only one reason, for Lou to call me into his office and that was to tell me I was being optioned back to Louisville where I could get steady work starting every fourth day. Okay, I could live with that, probably benefit from it. After all, the only way to gain experience pitching is to pitch.

My thoughts quickly shifted to Betty and Rusty and how we were going to manage traveling by car from Boston to Louisville with a very sick child. I prepared myself for the worst and headed to the manager's office to face the news, good or bad. It turned out to be both. The good news was I was not being optioned to Louisville. Instead, Lou told me I was going to start the first game. Clevenger, who was scheduled to start, took sick. That's the bad news. I don't like to benefit from someone else's misfortune, but that's life in the majors. It's life anywhere!

For the second time that day, my focus shifted, from no longer thinking about transporting my wife and sick child to Louisville to thoughts about facing a veteran Baltimore lineup. Fate had dumped an opportunity in my lap. It's said that opportunity only knocks once. The question was would I be able to seize the moment? If not, most likely, I could still be on my way to Louisville the next day. It was not, in the broad sense of the word, a win-or-else situation, but major league baseball teams would not allow their top young prospects to sit idle on the bench. One must play to learn the game of baseball, especially at the top level. Developing players is the lifeblood of future pennant winning teams, and young pitchers need to pitch and pitch often in order to gain the necessary skill to perform at the major league level. With this in mind, there was pressure on me to pitch well.

I had not pitched in a game in ten days. Usually this resulted in my fastball riding high in the strike zone rather than low. That's bad news for a sinkerball pitcher. My warm-up prior to the game proved me right! I would really have to concentrate to keep my pitches down in the zone. If I didn't, it could still end up being a short summer in Boston.

As we took to the field, 35,000 hysterical Red Sox fans leaped to their feet, arms flaring, and voices screaming. This was their team; they lived and died with every pitch of every game. It was true love multiplied 35,000 times! The National Anthem sprang from the speakers. I was standing on the mound at Fenway Park, preparing to make my first Major League start. Ted Williams, who was now back in the line-up after his injury, pranced in left field, keeping loose. Jimmy Piersall roamed in center doing what Jimmy did, which at any given time could be interesting. Jensen waited calmly in right field. My eyes wandered across the infield. Harry Agganis, the former All-American quarterback from Boston College, was at first base. Ted Lepcio, who played his college baseball at Seton Hall, was at second. Milt Bolling, a Southern gentleman from Alabama, covered shortstop and the veteran Grady Hatton, from Texas, was at third.

The call," Play Ball," bellowed from the throat of home plate umpire Bill Summers. I turned to face Baltimore's lead-off hitter, Al Abrams. The veteran right fielder pointed the head of the bat toward the mound. It was his way of saying, "Okay rookie, let's see what you got." I took the fastball sign from catcher Sammy White, went into my windup, and let it fly right down the middle. Strike one! The dream that was born on the sandlots in Pittsburgh had carried me this far the question now was, but how long would the dream last?

I thought back to the meeting I had with White and one of the coach's prior to the game, when we shared a quick run-down on the Baltimore hitters. Abrams liked the ball on the inside of the plate. White signaled for another fastball and set up on the outside corner of the plate. The pitch started down the middle then sank away from Abrams. He grounded weakly to Lepcio at second. Eddie Waitkus lifted a foul ball behind the plate that White gathered in for the second out. Bob Diering walked on six pitches. Up to the plate stepped Vern Stephens, the former great third baseman of the Red Sox. Stephens was big, strong and powerful. He could hit the ball out of any park in America, including Yellowstone. I fooled him with a sharp breaking ball on the first pitch and he grounded back to the mound to end the inning. One inning down, eight innings to go.

Bolling opened Boston's half of the first with a base on balls, but was stranded when Piersall struck out. Williams lined to second. White popped up behind home plate to end the inning. The Orioles went down in order in the second and third. To open the third inning, Bolling fanned then Piersall flied to right. Williams followed with a line shot to right field. White walked. Jensen lined a double into the gap in right-center, scoring Williams and White. With first base open, the left-handed hitting Agganis was walked, but Lepcio grounded to short to end the inning.

Nursing a two-run lead, I walked Diering to open the Baltimore fourth. Two pitches later, he attempted to steal second, but White picked up the Baltimore steal sign and threw Diering out with room to spare. Stephens grounded to short, and Sam Mele grounded weakly to third to close out the inning. Piersall opened our half of the inning with a home run into the screen in left to up the lead to 3-0 through four innings.

I was feeling good at this stage of the game. My fastball was in the upper 90s, my breaking ball was sharp, and I had a good change off the fastball. I was keeping the Oriole hitters off balance. Normally a pitcher is not aware of the mood of the crowd but for some reason I was on this day. When the game started, the fans were probably curious. Who was this kid from the minors? How long would he survive the bats of Stephens, Mele, Waitkus, Clint Courtney, and the rest of the veteran Oriole line-up? As we moved into the top of the fifth inning, the curiosity changed to wonder as the best the Orioles could do was pick up a base on balls sandwiched around a soft fly to right, a ground ball to second, and a strikeout. In the sixth, the wonder turned to ovation as the Orioles were turned back to the bench — hitless.

Mele opened the seventh inning for Baltimore and with the count three and two, lifted an easy fly ball near the foul line in left. The "Green Monster" stands just 315 feet from home plate. Williams, who played the wall better than anyone in the league, moved over to make the catch. He leaped at the last moment and the ball hit just over his outstretched glove, a single that ended my dream of a no-hitter. Courtney popped to second, Bobby Young flied to shallow center, and Billy Hunter grounded to second to end the inning. I was still too pumped up to feel any despair over losing the no-hitter, but I sure wanted the shutout and I wanted it badly!

In the eighth for the Orioles, Abrams grounded to short for the first out. Waitkus lifted a soft Texas leaguer behind second that Lepcio took on the run for out number two. Gil Coan, hitting for Howie Fox, who had relieved Bob Turley in the sixth, skied softly to Jensen in right. Eight innings down, one more to go.

In the Baltimore ninth, Diering grounded to short. Stephens took a third strike for out number two. Then Mele, who broke up the no-hitter, stepped to the plate. Baseball is a simple game, hitters are paid to hit and pitchers are paid to get them out. Most of it's impersonal. At least it was in this case; however, I was pumped up. I wanted that shutout in my first start more than I thought and I wasn't about to allow Mr. Mele to reach base again. I fooled him with a curveball for strike one. Most likely he was looking for me to lay a fastball down the middle. The Boston fans were up on their feet cheering. They could sense the kill. I was not about to disappoint them or me. I reached back and threw my best fastball of the day, and Mele took the pitch for strike two. I was sure he was looking for me to finish him off with another curve but he guessed wrong. White signaled for me to waste a breaking ball. For the first time that day I shook off the sign. I was learning to read the hitters, he was looking for the curveball. I ended the game the way I started it, a fastball on the outside corner, knee high. Strike three!

I walked off the mound to a standing ovation from the same crowd that was silent in wonder just two hours before. Will I ever forget that Sunday afternoon at Fenway Park? No, not ever. The crowd was jubilant. My teammates and coaches were estatic. But the biggest thrill of the day came when my boyhood idol, Williams walked over to my locker, took me by the hand and said, "Great job, kid, a hell of a great job!"

Betty did not know that I had pitched or what the final score was until one of the wives called her. That evening we managed to have a quiet family celebration of pizza and soft drinks. She was too exhausted to cook or go out, and Rusty was feeling better but not well enough to leave with a baby-sitter. She retired early. I was still far too keyed-up to even think about sleeping. I sat quietly in the dark, reliving one of the most exciting days of my life, most certainly of my baseball career. It was a long journey from the oil-soaked fields at Pittsburgh's Peabody High School, where the journey began, to Boston's Fenway Park. I dozed off with pleasant thoughts of how and when the dream began and wondered how it would end. One thought kept ringing in my head: "Great job, kid, a hell of a great job!"

I soon learned what the consequences were of having nine newspapers in one town. Each paper had to find a way to deal with the same game, make it interesting enough to sell papers and at the same time mention the score. One paper had this heart-warming story of how my sick three-year-old son had seen me pitching on television and crawled out to the kitchen to get his mother to watch the game. Another told a story of how general manager Joe Cronin ripped up my contract and doubled my salary. One related that the Red Sox owner Tom Yawkey had given me a bonus check for $1,000. They all sounded great! Sadly enough, none of them were true.

I was a dreamer as a kid — still am. I remembered reading these wonderful adjective-filled, descriptive stories of sporting events. I loved the flowing rhyme of Grantland Rice and others such writers. People see things for different reason and in various contexts. To most, a sporting event is just that, nothing more. To others it opens a beautiful passageway high above the everyday realm in which it took place. Such was my feeling a few days later when I picked up the Boston Daily Record and read an article by Dave Egan that transposed the commonness of a baseball game, by use of the gifted pen, and lifted it far beyond the baseball diamond. The article was headlined "Kemmerer's Effort A Dream Come True." This is how Egan interpreted my first start.

❝It always has seemed to me that the freedom to dream bold and confident dreams is the most priceless of all the freedoms, if only because it includes all of them. To dream of going to the church of one's choice, however small and insignificant it may be. Of speaking one's piece in a lost, lonely, and unpopular cause, of having a roof over one's head and food on one's table, and a little piece of land by the side of the road or waking unafraid through life, a free citizen in a free country, freedom of religion and speech; and freedom from fear and want. Those are the big goals, and they are all included in the freedom to dream, but there is more than this in my favorite freedom.

This is a better America than it was ten years ago, if only because the dreams of our colored kids now have wider horizons. Given athletic ability, they can now fight their way to security. They always were permitted and encouraged to box, and through this is in some respects of the ugliest of our sports, it must be said for it that it blazed the trail in the democratic processes for other sports to follow. Now the little ones in our colored population can dream brave, confident dreams of playing big-league football and basketball and baseball. The gateway of opportunity for all in the field of sports, and it is good to be a part of the panorama that needs not weasel and does not have to make lame and phony excuses for denying to others the rights we demand of ourselves.

Cold Confident Dream Comes True

Little did I think that anything of such a serious nature would come off today's typewriter, but that's the way it is with a man who writes for a living. He sits down and puts his index finger on the keyboards and the words rush out, marshalling themselves into sentences and paragraphs. Sometimes they laugh, and sometimes they weep, and sometimes they come out mad as hell, but the man who writes them has little control over them. They are their own bosses. Today's column started innocently enough, when I saw Russ Kemmerer pitch a one- hit shutout in his first major league start. Here was a bold, confident dream, being made good in a bold and confident manner, and young Russ Kemmerer gave me one of the unforgettable hours of my life.

In this business, thrills get to be a quarter a dozen after a man's been at it long enough. Oh, he retains his capacity for being thrilled, and if he doesn't he should look for a new job, but it becomes impossible to sort them out and say that here, on this particular day or night in this particular city was one of the great thrills. So it is sufficient to say that I shall not forget Russ Kemmerer and his debut as a starting pitcher.

It was a sweet, warm Sunday afternoon in July, and the game itself was almost completely unimportant. The Red Sox have in mind the modest goal of fourth place. The Orioles are bent on escaping eighth place. The big battles of the league were being fought elsewhere, so far away that the clamor of the heavy artillery and the flashes of gunfire could not be heard over the intervening hills or seen on the horizon. It was just another ballgame until Russ Kemmerer came along to make it a very special occasion, for it was an occasion on which the dreams of millions of American boys come true.

Heaved Into the Breach at the Last Moment

He was heaved into the breach at the last moment, and this always is the part of the dream. He was going against the highly publicized "Bullet-Bob" Turley, and this also is part of any dream that is worth its salt. Completely unknown, he stood in front of the crowd that pitied him and wondered how long he'd survive the bats of Stephens and Mele and Courtney and the grizzled gorillas of the opposition. But the pity turned to curiosity, and the curiosity to wonder, and the wonder to ovation, as inning after inning he turned them back to the bench defeated. So finally in the seventh inning, Mele hit one off the scoreboard just out of Williams reach, a hit in this ballpark, but he took a hitch in his pants and grabbed the ball and went back to work again and fought for his shutout and struck out two of the three men who faced him in the ninth, and it was a good feeing, to walk off the mound at the end of the top of the ninth and to receive a standing ovation from the same thousands who had pitied him two hours earlier.

I thank Russ Kemmerer for giving me such a glowing afternoon while making the average boys dreams come true, and I thank him in particular because my 11-year-old boy was with me. He will remember this warm, soft, Sunday afternoon as long as he lives, and long after I'm gone, he'll think fondly of his old man, sitting side by side in Fenway Park on the day that Russ Kemmerer gave substance and vitality to a wonderful dream. **99**

Boston Red Sox 4, Baltimore Orioles 0 - July 18, 1954

Baltimore	ab	r	h	rbi	Boston	ab	r	h	rbi
Abram, rf	3	0	0	0	Bolling, ss	3	0	0	0
Waitkus, 1b	3	0	0	0	Piersall, rf	4	1	1	1
Diering, cf	2	0	0	0	Williams, lf	4	1	1	0
Stephens, 3b	4	0	0	0	White, c	3	1	1	1
Mele, lf	4	0	1	0	Jensen, cf	3	0	2	2
Courtney, c	3	0	0	0	Agganis, 1b	4	0	2	0
Young, 2b	3	0	0	0	Lepcio, 2b	4	0	1	0
Hunter, ss	2	0	0	0	Hatton, 3b	3	0	1	0
Turley, p	1	0	0	0	Kemmerer, p	2	1	1	0
Coan, ph	1	0	0	0	**Totals**	**30**	**4**	**9**	**4**
Fox, p	0	0	0	0					
Total	**26**	**0**	**1**	**0**					

E - Bolling. 2B - Jensen, Hatton. 3B - Jensen, Agganis. HR - Piersall, White. Sac - Turley. DP - Baltimore 1, Boston 1. Left on base - Baltimore 5, Boston 8. Bases on balls - off Turley 5, Fox 1, Kemmerer 5. Struck out - by Turley, 5, Fox 1, Kemmerer 4. Winning pitcher - Kemmerer (1-0). Losing pitcher - Turley (7-10). Time of game 1:56.

After my near-miss no-hitter, I lost a 2-1 decision against Cleveland when Jensen misjudged a fly ball. Then I won the last American League game at Philadelphia's old Shibe Park. The Athletics moved to Oakland before the next season began.

My rookie season was by far the most exciting year of my life. The only major league baseball park that I had actually been in before then was Forbes Field in Pittsburgh. I had seen pictures of Yankee Stadium, the Polo Grounds, Comiskey Park, and a few of the old ballparks. My first season was special for a number of reasons: every city we traveled to was a new experience for me, the people were different than those I was use to in Pittsburgh, and each city had great places to see and visit. Every ballpark had it legends, history and a unique army of loyal fans that live and die with their heroes.

Yankee Stadium was at the top of my personal list. I could hardly wait to see "The House That Ruth Built." I was almost breathless as I walked from the visitor's locker room through the tunnel that led to the playing field. I stood on the top step of the visitor's dugout and looked out over the most noted baseball diamond in the history of the game. You could almost feel the ghost of former heroes drifting out to their positions waiting for the cry of play ball to echo throughout the stadium. More than the ghost of Babe Ruth and Lou Gerhig were in the stadium this particular day. It was Old Timers Day, and many Hall of Fame players of the past were there in person to be honored for their contributions to the great American pastime. I was on the field and in the same dugout talking with George Sisler, Bill Terry, Frankie Frisch, Mel Clark, Gabby Hartnett, Charles Gehringer, Pie Traynor, Lefty Grove, Joe Cronin, Carl Hubbell, Joe DiMaggio, Paul Waner, Jimmy Foxx, Rogers Hornsby, Bump Hadley, and Hank Greenberg. It was truly my "Field of Dreams" experience. Never in my wildest imagination did I ever even think of being on the same field with so many of the greatest players to ever play the game. This fantastic day will remain as clear in my mind as it was that day, and I will always cherish the baseball they signed for me as long as I live.

Williams was entering the twilight of his brilliant career. Nagging injuries kept him from playing in the early part of the season, and he was rounding into shape. The Yankees radio broadcaster, Mel Allen, introduced each of the former players. When he had finished the introductions he said, "Ladies and gentlemen I would like to take a moment more to introduce one more great player who will most certainly be inducted into the Hall of Fame in future years, Ted Williams." He loped out to home plate, and tipped his cap as the crowd applauded. The depth of it all suddenly swelled up inside, an unashamed tear trickled down my cheek. A lump the size of a baseball in my throat, made it almost impossible to swallow. I realized that by the Grace of God, I was granted a small part of this great games expanding history. Ted returned to the dugout and I believe I saw a tear trickle down his cheek. I was blessed to be on the field that day with these greats of the past, and have the opportunity to play for the next decade with and against players who would later be inducted into the Hall of Fame.

My greatest experience in baseball was not a personal accomplishment, but experiencing the privilege to play in the major leagues with many of the greatest to ever ware the uniforms. My goal was to be a major league baseball player. I now realize that goals are nothing more than dreams with deadlines.

One trip that was out of the ordinary was to the Polo Grounds to play the New York Giants in an exhibition game. Like most exhibition games played in those days, the purpose was to raise money for some good cause and to give the home fans a quick look at a team from the other league. The regulars from each team usually played about three innings before giving way to the utility players.

One event that was almost always scheduled for these games was a home run hitting contest pitting the sluggers from one team against the other. It turned out to be anything but a routine evening. Both clubs took batting and infield practice, and then the homerun contest took place. Representing the Giants were Dusty Rhodes, Hank Thompson, Monte Irvin, and Willie Mays. The Red Sox countered with Agganis, Gernert Jensen, and Williams. Each player would hit five fair balls. The player who hit the most home runs would be declared the winner.

The Giants led off with Rhodes who hit one into the seats in right field. Thompson followed with one homer to left field. Irvin hit two balls into the seats, followed by Mays who lofted three homers into the stands.

Gernet led off for the Sox and hit one ball into the seats. Agganis followed with one homer. Jensen drilled two balls into the stands. Then Williams moved from the dugout and stepped toward home plate. A hush fell over the crowd as he stepped into the on-deck circle. A feeling of expectation hung in the air. Ted looked at a couple of pitches from Paul Schreiber, our bullpen coach and batting practice pitcher, then lined his next pitch into the lower deck. Schreiber delivered again and Ted pulled it just inside the foul pole for homer number two. Williams took a couple of pitches that were not to his liking then smashed Paul's next offering into the upper deck. The crowd was on its feet and players from both teams moved to the top step of the dugouts. Schieber delivered his next pitch, and Williams, with that perfect swing, lofted one high and far into the deep recesses of the upper deck. The fans stood silent for a moment as the ball left the bat then they exploded as it settled into the seats. Four swings, four home runs. Could the greatest hitter in the game make it five for five? Ted took the next pitch, which was low. Paul delivered! At first it appeared that the ball would clear the roof and leave the ballpark. For a moment everything seemed to be in slow motion! The ball arched high into the sky, smashed just below the light towers and rocketed into the stands. The fan and players stood in a standing ovation that lasted five minutes. Unbelievable! I've never seen anything like it and most likely never will.

The year that began with such high hopes for the Red Sox finished in mediocrity, a fourth place with a record of 69 and 85. Cleveland ran away from the league and set a record with 111 victories. Most of the decisions made by the Boston brass turned sour. The veterans didn't produce and the heralded prospects fell short of their expectations. In many cases Boston gave up far too soon on many of these young players, who later developed and went on to have good careers with other teams. In defense of the decisions the Red Sox made regarding the talented, young players one needs to consider the fact that there were only eight major league teams in each league. This made it necessary for the front office to make quick decisions on the development of players and this involved more luck than judgment. One other fact needs to be considered. The philosophy on young players at this time was that it took several years for a player to develop and there was not room on the major league roster to keep all of them. Boudreau was let go as the Red Sox skipper, and the building project was destined to start over again. The one really bright spot in the year was Williams. Fully recovered from his broken collarbone, he played in 117 games, hit 29 home runs, drove in 89 runs, and hit .345. He went to bat 386 times, just short of the required 400 times at bat to qualify for the batting title. The 400 times at-bat rule did not include base on balls or sacrifice flies. Ted drew 136 bases on balls and would have given him another batting title had the rule not existed. Three years later in 1957, the rule was changed to read, "A hitter must have 477 total plate appearances including walks, times hit by pitches and sacrifices."

The year that began with such great hope ended in despair. On the other hand, I ended the season winning five, losing three with an earned run average of 3.84. I felt good about my future in baseball.

Chapter 5
Winter Ball

After the 1954 season, Mike Higgins, who had piloted the Red Sox AAA farm team to the American Association championship, was hired as the new Boston manager. One of his goals was to develop and use the wealth of minor league talent in the organization's farm system.

A few days before the season ended, outfielder Faye Throneberry and I were called to the front office. Joining us was one of our coaches, Mickey Owens. General manager Joe Cronin explained that Mickey was going to coach the Ponce team in the Puerto Rican winter baseball league. They wanted Faye and me to play on the team. Cronin said it would be great experience and help us develop the skills we needed to improve.

Throneberry needed to learn to hit the breaking ball, and I needed work on changing speeds.

In early October, my wife Betty, our son Rusty, and I headed for Puerto Rico. We landed at the Santucy Airport and were instructed to take a public taxi across the island to Ponce, which would be our home for the season. We had to travel over the mountains. The roads were dirt and just about wide enough to accommodate two small cars. Ninety percent of the curves were ninety degree. Whenever we approached a curve, the driver would blow the horn but maintain his speed. A large percentage of the time we were on the left side looking over the valley that lay a thousand feet below. I would list this trip as the most harrowing of my entire life. My wife and I were stark white and scared stiff. Rusty, on the other hand, enjoyed every moment. I have never been so overjoyed to rest my feet on solid ground as I was that day. The drive took over three hours and I truly believe it was only by the grace of God that we arrived safely. I have been on several frightening journeys in my day, but I have never experienced the outright fear that I did during that trip.

We soon learned that not only was Ponce at the tail end of the island, but it was the tail end of everything. The ballpark was run down, the uniforms were hand-me-downs from the 1927 Yankees, and transportation did not exist. On the positive side, the owners did provide us with a house. We found it impossible to find any food that looked appetizing, with the exception of the fantastic freshly baked bread that was sold daily from a street push cart that promptly stopped in front of our home each day at 3 p.m. We quickly discovered several major facts that would influence our lifestyle. The windows had no glass, only vents, so it was necessary to sleep under netting because of the mosquitoes. An abundance of playful salamanders roamed freely about the premises. And we had to race to the bank every payday because of a shortage of funds to meet the payroll. One might say, it was a first-come, first-serve situation. That we never missed a paycheck might be considered a minor miracle.

Faye and I solved the transportation problem with the help of the Puerto Rican players. We purchased a small, used motorbike that had a seat for the driver and a second seat over a compartment for the passenger. The compartment was used to store our equipment as we drove to the ballpark. It was also useful for grocery shopping and to take our wives, one at a time, on short sight-seeing trips to town.

Once the season began, we settled into the environment and developed a routine that was more familiar to us. Baseball is the same game regardless of where it is played. Part of our daily routine, when we played at home, was to crank up the motorbike and head for the ballpark each day at 5 p.m. We wound our way through the streets that had speed bumps placed every one hundred feet to control the almost non-existent traffic. People would sit on small porches and the adults as well as the kids would wave to us and call out our names, pronounced in broken English with a Spanish accent, "Que, Passé, Cemmarraro, Throngberry." We soon accepted our adopted names. Their love of baseball was unmatched and formed a solid foundation for the popularity that transcended nationality and language barriers. The wonderful, smiling, happy, friendliness of the people is something that lingers in my mind to this day.

The baseball team, like most things in Ponce, was at the tail end of the standings. People crowded the park each night and cheered us on regardless of the outcome. Some of the larger towns could afford four top players from the states, which was the limit of American players on each team. Ponce had Faye and me. We held our own, winning some, losing some, never being embarrassed, but holding up the rest of the teams in the standings. The schedule called for a sixty-game season that ran from mid-October to the first week in January. The quality of the league could be measured somewhere between Double-A and Triple-A baseball. We ended up winning about thirty-two games. The season was, however, far from a failure for Faye and me. Faye learned to hit the curve ball, and I learned to change speed on my pitches. He was near the top of the league in hitting and I was high on the list of winning pitchers with nine victories.

One thing I had trouble accepting when I went to town is people reaching out to touch me. The touching wasn't offensive, but I wondered why it was happening. I also noticed that it did not occur every time I walked around town, only on certain days. Finally, I asked the Puerto Rican players. They told me that the people thought I was lucky and that touching me would bring them luck. By some rare coincidence, a famous racehorse on the island was named Cammerraro, which just happened to be how my name would be spelled and pronounced in Spanish. Cammerraro had won 53 straight races, and if by chance he was running in a race and I was pitching on the same day, people would touch me for luck and they would bet Cammerraro to win his race and the Ponce team to win the baseball game. They believed that together we held some mystic power over the god of luck, and winning was a certainty. I guess I should have taken it as a sign of honor, but in all truthfulness, I couldn't help think of what end of the horse I would be if I lost my end of the bargain.

As it turned out, I would need more than luck before the season ended. I pitched a complete game one night. If my memory serves me correctly, it was a shutout and an easy game. I don't recall hurting my arm during the game, but the next morning when I got out of bed, I couldn't raise my arm high enough to comb my hair. I treated it with heat packs during the day, but by the time I arrived at the ballpark and dressed for the game, I still could not throw the ball twenty feet. I told Owens that I most likely slept with my arm under me, and it would be okay in a few days. Players in my generation seldom revealed injuries of this nature to management. Injured ball players were of no value to the team and more or less guaranteed a ticket to the minor leagues or out of baseball.

Secretly, I decided the following day to go the hospital. My shoulder was just as sore as it had been the day before and I wanted to get some treatment while still keeping the injury quiet. The treatment I received at the hospital helped slightly, but I began to doubt if I would be able to pitch in three days when my next start was scheduled. This was the first time in my life that I had a sore arm or any other athletic injury. I was depressed! I walked to the hospital, but on my return trip home I somehow took a wrong turn.

Suddenly, I found myself standing in front of a Catholic Church. In the courtyard was a statue of Jesus Christ on the cross. I began to weep. I thought if this arm didn't heal, my baseball career could be over. I was not Catholic, but I had been brought up in the church. My parent's had been German Lutheran, but by the time I was born they were attending the Methodist Church. I believe my athletic ability through faith enabled me to play baseball, and I believed that through my faith I would continue my baseball career.

I entered the church, dropped to my knees, and with tears streaming down my cheeks, asked God to heal my arm. I told him that if he would heal me and give me back my career, I would be faithful to him for the remainder of my life. I told my wife the story of stopping to pray at the church. We shared a quiet prayer together putting the past behind us and began to believe in His direction for the future.

I missed one turn in the pitching rotation. I found out that if I stretched really well and took about twenty minutes to warm up, I was able to throw with good speed. I also found out how to rely more on my breaking ball and changing speeds rather than relying on sheer power to get hitters out. The arm hurt for the rest of the season, and I looked forward to returning home and resting for a short month before reporting to spring training with the Red Sox.

Over the course of the last forty years or so, I have given much thought to those days in Puerto Rico and the injury to my arm. I have reached the conclusion that certain things are supposed to happen. Without these detours changing our attitude and often the directions in our lives, it is evident that we would have missed many of the feature happenings in our life that, if given a choice we would not have missed for anything in the world. The problem is that we only see today, this hour, this minute; God sees the whole lifespan.

The baseball season ended in Puerto Rico on January 5, 1955. I had about five weeks until the Red Sox opened spring training in Sarasota, Florida. I prayed that the advice and treatment I would be able to obtain in Pittsburgh would heal my shoulder and have me at full strength by the opening of training camp. From a pure pitching perspective, the season in Puerto Rico had helped me accomplish what I had gone there to learn, changing speeds, and using my breaking ball to set up my fast ball. If I had not injured my arm I would have been extremely satisfied with nine wins and three loses with a last-place ball club.

From that point on, my daily prayer was that the shoulder would heal, and I would be back to normal by the time spring training opened on February 15. I had no doubt about God's willingness to answer prayers! I also believe that they're answered in three ways: yes, no, and wait. We are impatient beings that demand immediate response. Not only do we pray for a specific request, but we also outline for Him how and when we want it to come about. On the other hand, God's timing is perfect; he's never late!

I was advised by Boston to simply rest the arm, stretch the shoulder, and apply alternating heat then cold compresses three times a day. I followed this routine faithfully. I also ran three miles every morning and worked out with several of the Pirate players at the East Liberty YMCA. I reported to spring training in great physical shape. I tipped he scale at a solid 220 and ready to take on the challenge of winning my spot on the pitching staff. My mental attitude was good. I was raring to go. The pitchers and catchers reported to camp two weeks before the rest of the team. The purpose was to get our arms and bodies in shape prior to the full squad reporting on March first. We ran, fielded bunts, worked on throwing to various bases, covering first base on balls hit to the left side of the infield, and pitch location. Once the whole team was in camp we would be throwing twenty minutes of batting practice every other day until the Grapefruit League games began with other teams training in Florida.

Everything went well during the drills, but after throwing batting practice a few times, the shoulder felt better but the pain was still there. By the time the Grapefruit League season ended my shoulder was feeling better. I pitched well enough to make the team and head back to Boston for the opening of the season.

The first month of the season I was used sparingly, mostly in relief. I started two games, was credited with one win and one loss, but my numbers were not very impressive — 17 innings, 15 base on balls and 13 strikeouts, and a horrible ERA of 7.41.

Manager Higgins called me into his office. "You're not throwing the ball like you use to," he explained. "We noticed it during spring training, but we thought you were tired from pitching over 100 innings in Puerto Rico, so we decided to limit your batting practice and innings pitched in spring training in hopes you'd regain the fastball, but it just has not happened. We want you to go back to Louisville to see if more work in the warm weather will bring you around. You'll have time to work it out until you're ready to come back."

Looking back on that year, the thing that surprised me the most was they knew there was something wrong with the arm, Owens must have told them about my arm problem, yet there was never even the slightest suggestion of sending me to a doctor for an examination to see if the injury could be repaired. Today, players who have injuries are given all kinds of tests to evaluate their physical ability thanks to modern medicine and procedures like Tommy John surgery. Actually, I'm to blame, I could have told them about the injury, but I didn't!

So once again I packed my bags and headed for Louisville to try again to regain what I had lost. Everyone who has ever lived has experienced setbacks in life that cause major alterations in the direction they travel. Sometimes those changes bring on disaster, like the prominent physician that ended up on skid-row because he could not deal with the reality of losing a young life on the operating table. For all of us there are times when it is difficult to keep our chin up. I constantly reminded myself the God has not given us the spirit of fear, but of love and peace and a sound mind. I never lost faith that I would be able to continue my career. We cannot base our lives on our feelings alone, or what we see, because these constantly change, but faith in a God, who knows us better than we know ourselves and provides the stability that the Apostle Paul suggested, "Be content in whatever state you are in and hold tightly to your faith."

The ball club at Louisville was better than average and I believed that with a few good outings under my belt I'd be on my way back. The problem was it never happened! It wasn't so much the physical problems as it was the mental. My wife Betty was carrying our second child; as a result she was at home in Pittsburgh with her parents. She had a rare blood type that made delivering a child a little risky. Besides, I missed my family. I needed to turn to dad or one of my bothers, just to chat and get a little tender loving care. Actually, my big hang-up was I had lost all confidence in my ability to pitch. This happens often to athletes in every sport; it strikes in every area of life. In most cases it takes just one or two good outings to regain your stability and get you back on track. It just never happened for me. I'd have a good outing followed by a mediocre game, and then a disaster! At times I felt as if I was learning to pitch all over again, the confidence never returned. I finished the season with a 5-6 record and an earned run average of 4.96. These were the worst numbers I had ever posted in pro ball. The best thing that happened that year was Betty gave birth to our second child, Cheryl Leigh, on July 10th. Both mother and daughter came through the experience in great shape. Betty and I were pleased that we now had a son and a daughter.

When the season ended I headed back home to Pittsburgh with a cloud of despair hanging over me. The pitchers who had replaced me on the Red Sox had performed reasonably well, and I knew it would take a supreme effort for me to restore the confidence in me that the front office had lost. My thoughts: keep the faith!

I reported to spring training February 15, 1956, feeling that the Red Sox front office had little thought of including me in the pitching rotation.

I felt good the first couple of weeks, my arm was strong, and I was throwing well, but when the exhibition games began my name was seldom in the lineup. I pitched an inning or two here and there and did well, but I certainly was not receiving the attention I had hoped for from the coaching staff.

The Red Sox had changed Triple-A affiliates; Louisville of the American Association was no longer their top farm club. San Francisco of the Pacific Coast League, the best league in the minors, would take that spot. For many years, players in the PCL would refuse to come to the majors because they could make more money on the coast. I believe Boston had promised to bring a winning team to the city. As a result, the best players they had in their system were sent to Frisco. I had one option remaining and the Red Sox wanted to see if a year in the coast league would help me regain the promise I showed my rookie season. I was disappointed to be returning to the minor leagues, but at the same time I was determined to show them that my fastball had returned and I was ready to claim my place on the pitching staff. Also, there was still the unanswered prayer that I had not forgotten and I was positive it had not slipped God's mind either.

The Pacific Coast League was everything I was told it would be. Big cities, such as Los Angeles, San Francisco, Hollywood, and Seattle, made every road trip exciting. More major league caliber ball players were here than in the American Association, which featured mainly prospects. The main difference in the schedule of the two leagues was that the coast league played more day games, which was great for me because the heat made it easier for me to get loose.

All in all, the season was good for me. Joe Gordon was a super manager. I learned more baseball from him, especially about hitting, than I thought existed. I ended up winning 14 games and losing 12 with an earned run average of 3.48 — not bad with a ball club that finished in sixth place in the standings. I had three highlights during the season. First, I stopped Steve Bilko's hitting streak at 45 games. Secondly, I was selected to the North All-Star team, and I was the winning pitcher in the game. Finally, and most important, my arm felt good, still a little sore at times, but better. My fastball was back in the mid-nineties. When the season ended, I headed back to Pittsburgh with confidence that I had performed well enough to impress the Red Sox to take a close look at me in the spring and reserve a spot for me on the roster.

I was out of options, because the Red Sox had sent me to the minors three times, so they would have to keep me, trade me, sell me or put me on waivers. The waiver list gave every other major league team a chance to claim the services of this player for a reasonable, predetermined waiver fee of a dollar. If no other major league team claimed the player within the three-day period, the parent club could release, sell, or trade his contract to any team, either major or minor league, but he would no longer remain the property of the team that formerly owned him. Clubs often used the waiver list as a means of finding out what other teams' interest in certain players was in order to negotiate a trade. This was possible because clubs had the option under the waiver rule to withdraw a player's name at any time during the three-day waiver period. It was common practice for baseball teams to use the you-scratch-my-back-I'll-scratch-yours method of getting players through waivers. I felt confident that based on my winning rookie season and the success I had at San Francisco in 1956, there would be little chance of me clearing waivers.

My hopes of winning a roster spot became less and less of a possibility as spring training progressed. I was used sparingly, although I was with the club when training ended. Each club is permitted to carry twenty-eight men on the roster for thirty days for the first month of the season, after that they were committed to twenty-five players. During this period, I was used in one mop-up roll, without a decision. On April 29, I was notified that I had been traded along with Throneberry to the Washington for left-handed pitcher Dean Stone and right-handed reliever Bob Chakales. I was now a member of the Washington Senators — first in war, first in peace, and always it seemed, last in the American League. I was still in the major leagues but just by the skin of my teeth.

I joined the Senators in April 1957.

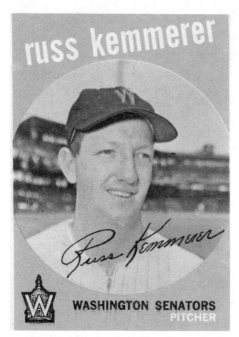

russ kemmerer

WASHINGTON SENATORS
PITCHER

My Topps card from 1959.

Chapter 6
The Senators

I joined the Senators in Cleveland. Charlie Dressen, who had great success managing the Brooklyn Dodgers, was the skipper and Walter "Boom-Boom" Beck was the pitching coach who taught me one of the greatest lessons I ever learned in life, which had nothing directly to do with baseball like a new pitch that would transform me into another Walter Johnson, but it did transform me. During my first season in Washington, Beck took me under his wing. I was his favorite boy and he did everything within his power to help me improve. He gave me the nickname of "Dutch" for two reasons. First, because he said I reminded him of a former great pitcher, Dutch Leonard, a 12-year veteran and a good friend of his. And he thought the nickname matched my German ancestry and temperament.

The team had settled into an eleven-game losing streak that was increased to twelve my first day with the team. The mood of the team was less than jovial as we returned to the hotel. The players quickly hurried off in small groups to have dinner with teammates and friends before returning to the hotel. It would be a short Friday night as Saturday and Sunday games were held in the afternoon in those days. I spent that evening with my new roommate, Dick "Snake" Hyde, a right-handed, submarine, relief pitcher. Dick filled me in on the good, bad, and indifference of the team.

I finally fell into a restless sleep, but was haunted by strange music and flashes of light. My subconscious mind informed me I was having a nightmare. I was dressed in my new Senator uniform bearing the number sixteen. I was sitting on a white jackass waving a red, white, and blue pennant inscribed, "Go Senators!" The pitching staff, dressed in black pin-stripped uniforms with fire-red hoods, and holding multi-colors torches aloft, chanted, *Take Me Out To The Ball Game*. They escorted me to the mound along with Dressen, who handed me the baseball and said, "Go get em kid!" I awoke in a cold sweat to what I thought was the sound of horsehide slamming into ash. In reality it was thunder. I turned over in bed quietly praying that we would be rained out.

Sure enough, it was raining the next morning and following breakfast the team reported to the ballpark and waited as the powers that be, the umpires, decided whether or not to call the game. We were informed of a mandatory team meeting at 6:30 o'clock that evening at the hotel. Being a newcomer on the club, and taking into consideration the current losing streak, I thought that perhaps, since we were rained out, we were going back to the hotel to have a victory party. Actually, it was just a front office plan to help the team relax by having a few drinks and a few laughs, while giving a few suggestions on breaking the losing trend. It didn't work! The losing streak continued. It reached fifteen before a victory came our way. A few days later, Dressen was fired as manager and Harry "Cookie" Lavagetto became the new manager. That's how I was introduced to Washington Senators baseball.

The 1957 Senators will not be noted in the record books as one of the most productive teams in its tradition filled history. We ended up losing 99 games while managing to win only 55. We played 154 games in those days. However, as so often is the case, strange and wonderful things develop from what first appears to be a disaster. Take the crucifixion of Jesus as a prime example. The foundation that would eventually result in a pennant winner was in place. Harmon Killebrew, Bob Allison, Bob Lemon, Camilo Pasqual, Jim Kaat, Pedro Ramos, and a few future additions would bring respectability to the organization, but the 1957 team as it stood was not in a class with the other seven teams in the American League. One might say the team was going through a transition stage. Calvin Griffith, the nephew and adopted son of Clark Griffith, had taken over the operation of the franchise and he was working hard to find available players with major league experience or those who might possibly add respectability to the team.

Killebrew, a future Hall of Fame player, was in the early stages of his development. Roy Sievers and Lemon, both stellar performers, added credibility to the offense and were valuable tutors for Harmon. The pitching staff had good potential with four quality starters. The veteran left-handed, Chuck Stobbs was the senior member of the staff followed by Pasqual and Ramos, a couple of class pitchers lifted out of Cuba. Truman Clevenger and myself were picked up from the Red Sox. Hyde and Ted Abernathy, a couple of right-handed submarine throwers, were tough customers coming out of the bullpen. Eddie Yost was a veteran third baseman. Pete Runnels was the Senator's most valuable player in 1956, leading the club in hits, doubles, and batting .310. Runnels broke the .300 hitting mark for the first time in his six-year career, and the Senators were looking for more of the same in 1957. He was converted from shortstop to second base making the move gracefully and allowing Rocky Bridges, a journeyman infielder picked up on wavers from Cincinnati, to move into the shortstop spot. Clint Courtney, who was picked up from Baltimore, Earl Batty, who joined us from the White Sox, and veteran Ed Fitzgerald completed the catching core. Herbie Plews was the utility infielder.

What the club lacked was experience, defense, and speed. We had trouble getting the big hits with runners in scoring position, and we lacked the speed to score base runners on routine hits. I contributed a little offense that season by knocking out two home runs. Both were against Kansas City. One was off Glen Cox in Kansas City and the other was off Alex Kellner in Washington. Both were two-run shots. I managed only one other hit that season. Defensively, we had difficulty turning the routine double play, and we lacked speed and good throwing arms in the outfield.

I was pleased with the opportunity to pitch regularly and be part of a starting major league pitching staff. I lost some close games and somehow managed to eke out seven wins with eleven loses that first season in Washington. I consider those lucky numbers because the Senators finished in last place. My ERA ended up at 4.95 on the season. My fastball returned my curveball and slip-pitch got better as the year progressed, and most of all my confidence returned. I lost eleven games, but all in all it was a great learning experience, and once again my future looked bright as a starting major league pitcher.

Being with the Senators after my stay with the Red Sox, to say the least, was dynamic. The Senators were a mixture of young talent, who like myself, were seeking to find a home in the big leagues. Besides the veterans, the majority of players were younger, having one to three years experience in the big leagues under their belts. Right off the bat you could feel a strong blending factor that would be an asset to the team. You had the fun guys: Hal Griggs, Whitey Herzog, Bridges, Hyde, and Courtney. Then there were the talented Cuban players: Jose Valdivelso, Julio Becqure, Carlos Paula, Pasqual, and Ramos. Then came a long list of hopefuls that Griffith brought in with designs to build a foundation for future Senator teams. Names like Killebrew, Plews, Throneberry, Milt Bolling, Bob Usher, and Art Schult. A wonderful blend of personalities.

What was lacking was the combination of talent, experience, and personality that would mold us into a team. We learned to laugh at and with each other when in reality we wanted to cry. We had a game won in the last inning and a routine grounder was hit to the infield that should have been fielded for the final out, but somehow it hit off the heel of the fielders glove and rolled up his sleeves. While he fought frantically to rip his shirt from his body to find the ball, the tying and winning runs scored from third and second. On another occasion an outfielder charged a line drive hit directly at him that should have ended the game. Instead, the ball nicked his glove for one error, hit the wall and as he turned to field the ball off the wall it went back through his legs for the second error on the play. He committed the third error when he picked up the ball and dropped it as he attempted to throw the runner out at home. When he finally did throw the ball it went twenty feet over the catcher's head for the fourth error on the play allowing the winning run to score. Four errors on one play must be some kind of record. The play was reminiscent of little league ball, not big league ball. Is it any wonder that we pushed toward the hundred loss mark?

Regardless of our pathetic win-loss record, the other seven teams in the league never took us for granted. Certainly there were games in which we got pounded or like the example I just used, simply made to many bad plays both physically and mentally to stay in the game, but on a day-to-day basis we had the pitching and hitting to be competitive. As a result teams didn't overlook us or write us off as easy pickings. Teams always played double-headers every Sunday, and many times teams threw a fifth starter at us in the second game, but for the most part they kept their regular four-man pitching rotation in order. Remember, only eight teams existed in each league, and as result players on every team got to know one another real well, so there were very few secrets — what you saw was what you got. Pitchers often discussed how they pitched to certain hitter and in return hitters discussed what pitchers were doing to get certain hitters out. Washington did show signs of promise. Runnels hit .310, Sievers and Bob Lemon combined for 56 home runs, the pitching staff made strides toward being solid. A couple of talented minor leaguers at Charlotte — Killebrew hit .325 with 15 home runs and Allison had size, speed, and power — impressed everyone. Griffith was adding talent that would prove vital to the team's future improvement.

The Senators were just about like every other team in the league when it came to personal relationships between players, roommates, families, and off-the-field interest. Teams tend to group together based on positions, personalities, interest and habits. For example, on road trips certain players liked to take in afternoon movies, while others liked to go to billiard parlors. Reading, sightseeing, and card playing were options. In Washington, we had a number of Spanish speaking players that sought out Spanish friends and restaurants when we traveled. Many times players went with them and developed a taste for Spanish food. As a general rule, the player's wives and family seem to match up in similar groups. Race and status was never an issue, it was always personal preference. The Senators did have one unique and very unusual group of players who liked to listen to and sing barbershop harmony.

Although wins were few, one thing that could be said for the 1958 Senators was we had harmony in the musical sense of the word. In spite of several outstanding individual performances, the team was all but out of the pennant race by the Fourth of July. While the team languished near the bottom of the league, a group of us gained instant notoriety when we entertained a national television audience in a musical performance. The group was made up of Clevenger, Sievers, Lemon, Albie Pearson, broadcaster Bob Wolff, and accordionist Howard Delvon, and me. We were called the Singing Senators.

My singing background started when I was a junior in high school. Three of my good friends on the football team and I began harmonizing in the shower after practice. It wasn't long before some of the players began to hang around after practice to listen to us. Someone suggested that we should sing a couple of numbers at the monthly high school dances that were held in the gym. So, Sam Ferrainola, Wilford Allen, Ervin Biggs, and I took the bull by the horns and volunteered our talents to the dance committee.

The school colors were maroon and gray, so the uniform pants the members of the band wore, were gray with a dark maroon strip on each leg. Our varsity sweaters were dark maroon with a large gray "P" trimmed in red and set on the left, lower side of the sweater. We added white shirts and a maroon tie. We had the perfect outfit for our first performance. We were popular and became regulars on the school dance program. We never

did try out for the Wilkins Amateur Hour, but we were invited back for the fifteenth class reunion.

So my interest in barbershop continued with the Singing Senators and became a feather in my cap when we were asked to perform on Dave Garroway's *Today* Show. On June 6 at six o'clock on the morning, we met at the Reflecting Pool, since our performance was at seven. The evening before, we had lost a 13-inning game to Kansas

My singing career began in high school with the Varsity Four. I had my head down for this photo.

68

City, 2-0, and didn't get to bed until long after one o'clock. Most of us got no more than three hours sleep, but by sunrise we were up to the musical challenge, and performed flawlessly. We were allotted a seven-minute slot on each of the three one-hour segments of the show. Among the numbers we sang were *For Me and My Gal, If you were a Tulip, Carolina in the Mornin*, and, of course, *Take Me Out to the Ballgame*. Pearson was also featured in his solo rendition of *Night and Day*.

Garroway's co-host, Jack Lescoulie, was on hand for the performance that morning and admitted that it was one of the longest spots ever granted by the program to a musical group. "They deserved it," he said. "They're that good!" By the next day they were the talk of their colleagues around the league.

The television show debut aired nearly two years after the group was originally formed. Wolff, a band leader and vocalist while a student at Duke University, used to sing for his supper outside the university dining hall. Remaining a music buff even after becoming the Senator's play-by play-voice, he would frequently bring his ukulele while traveling with the team on road trips. When some of the players began asking what he had in the case he was carrying around, he would whip out the uke and begin playing a few tunes. Several began singing along — at first informally — then with a little more fervor. That's when Wolff came up with the idea of actually forming a singing group among the players. Before long, crooning sessions were an integral part of the team's weekly schedule, especially on road trip where there was time to spare.

We also attracted attention when we performed at Griffith Stadium on a night honoring Sievers in September. We drew an encore applause from the crowd of more than 18,000, including Vice President Richard Nixon, who was on hand to pay tribute to his favorite player.

The group that sang on the *Today* show was not the original group. "We began fooling around with it in the early-to-mid Fifties," Wolff recalled. "As the Senators traded or released a player who happened to be in the group, we would scramble to find a suitable replacement. Competition for places in the group sometimes became pretty intense." At various times players such as Frank Shea, Julio Moreno, Usher, and Bolling were a part of the Singing Senators. When Bolling was traded to the Tigers prior to the 1958 season, he asked Wolff for advice in starting a similar group on the Detroit club.

The Singing Senators included (left to right) Howie Devlon, Truman Clevenger, Jim Lemon, Albie Pearson (front), me, Roy Sievers, Bob Wolff.

Not everyone who tried out of the group made it. When the club's public relations director, Herb Heft, announced that they had been invited to appear on the *Today* show, Wolff auditioned anyone on the team who had an interest and finally trimmed the group to five. "The competition became so heated that Cookie had to call a clubhouse meeting in Kansas City, so that Wolff could finally announce his selections and explain them as diplomatically as possible," Heft reported at the time. Not surviving the cut were Bob Malkmus, Norm Zauchin, Ramos, Hal Griggs, and Becquer.

Lavagetto was a supporter of the group while serving as a coach on the team, believing that such activities off the field helped to build esprit de corps among the players. When he became manager of the Senators, however, he took a somewhat sterner attitude. "I don't want them singing happy songs after losing a game," he said gruffly.

"There was no levity in losing," Wolff added, "but we would still rehearse. We just needed to be careful of where we did it. Sometimes we would go out in the woods to rehearse, and sometimes it would be in the men's room."

Although some viewed their act as novelty, the group took their singing as seriously as they took their baseball. Even though the level of their musical background varied — from singing in the shower or for fun, to performing in a musical and church choirs — they approached their music with an air of professionalism. Clevenger sang bass, Sievers and Wolff were tenors, and Lemon, Pearson and me sang the leads. Devon and Wolff provided musical accompaniment on the accordion and ukulele. They may not have been able to hit their way out of a paper sack, but they could sure carry a tune in a bucket.

One quality that elevated Wolff to the elite level of Hall of Fame broadcaster was his ability to relate and understand the inner feelings of the men he described day after day in his play-by-play broadcast and interview shows. Bob sought the real story. He might interview the star of the game, or more often than not, a player who made a contribution that won or saved a game, but not necessarily the home run or noticeable feat the fans would acknowledge. He was as friendly to the average player as he was to the stars on the team. One might argue that the team didn't have many stars, but that's not the case, he simply treated everyone with the same respect.

Being on a losing team might indicate to some that we were not serious enough about our playing, but that's just a poor evaluation of what professionalism really means. In the years since I finished my baseball career, I have been pleased to find out that the large majority of men I played with went on to be successful in what they were involved in after their baseball careers were over.

One such player was Pearson, a five-foot-five centerfielder who batted .275 and was clearly the outstanding rookie of the year in the American League. He certainly did not have the physical features that most baseball scouts are looking for today. But he did have heart and determination to go along with his talent. Pearson was the featured crooner and clearly the class of the vocal group. A few years earlier he sung with a vocal group of four girls. At his own wedding, he sang *Tenderly* and *Because* to his bride. A decade later, after his baseball career was over, he became a gospel recording artist for Impact Records, and was named the National Evangelical Film Foundation's Singer of the Year.

One noticeable difference between playing for the Boston Red Sox and the Washington Senators, other than their finishing position in the American League, was the demand on the player to make public appearances. Boston had the big names, such as Ted Williams, Johnny Pesky, Mel Parnell, and Dom DiMaggio, to name a few. There was seldom an opportunity for a rookie to make a personal appearance. Washington was another story. Every ballplayer, regardless of popularity or experience, was scheduled to make personal appearances to stir interest in the team, and to bring fans out to Griffith Stadium.

Howard Fox, the team's public relations director, was in charge of scheduling personal appearances. One day, he approached me with instructions and directions to St. Elizabeth's Hospital. He simply said they had a great group of Senator followers that would be delighted to have me say a few words and sign autographs. I pictured a ward of boys hungry to see a big league ballplayer.

The following day I found my way to the hospital. As I drove through the gates I became a little edgy when I passed a sign that read, St Elizabeth's Hospital, Mental Institution. I assumed that one might be a little crazy to be a Senator's fan, but I didn't expect them to carry it to this extreme.

I met the director and he accompanied me to a large room where there were a hundred or more people assembled. The majority of those in attendance had on hospital gowns, but there were a number of uniformed nurses, guards, doctors, and administrators.

I spoke to the administrator asked him if there was anything in particular he wanted me to mention? "Just say anything related to the Senators and baseball," he replied. These people have the mentally of five and six year old children. The truth is they're happy to have a major league player visit with them. It doesn't matter what you say." In Washington we were happy to be called a big league players, so I took his words as a compliment.

I began my talk telling them how happy I was to be one of the starting pitchers for the Senators. Suddenly, a man in a hospital gown stood up, and in a loud voice yelled, "Kemmerer, you're a bum!" That shook me up!

I turned to the director and he said, "Remember what I said about their mentality. Just go on with your comments."

I continued with my speech; however, in about five minutes the same gentleman stood up again and in a voiced that could clearly be heard by everyone in the room screamed, "Kemmerer, you haven't gotten anyone out in a month!"

This time it hurt me to hear these words of truth ringing around the room. I turned to the director once again, but before I could utter a word, I noticed a huge smile light up his face from ear to ear and he said in a loud voice. "Just go on with your speech. Do you realize that is the most intelligent words he's spoken since we've had him in here?" Such was life with the Washington Senators.

Back on the field, we were in New York for a series with the Yankees. It was one of those hot, humid days. I loved to pitch in the high humidity, because the heavy air affected my fastball and caused it to sink more than usual. The Yankees were having trouble and along about the third inning, Yankee coach Frankie Crossetti began to complain to the home plate umpire Bill Summers that I was throwing a spitball. My generation of pitchers were accused of doctoring the ball to make it do tricks. We were often accused of throwing the spitball or grease ball. I had a good sinking fastball that dived in hard toward a right-handed hitter, and broke down and away from a left-handed batter. This movement of my fastball resembled the action of a spitball. At times I was accused of throwing the wet one.

The big barrel-chested umpire, who was having trouble with the heat and humidity, strolled out to the mound to check my hat, head, hands, cap, and glove to see if I had any foreign substance that would make the ball do what it was doing.

"He's not using anything Frankie," Summers told him.

Crosetti's complaints continued through the fourth and fifth innings. Finally in the seventh, Frank complained one time too many times. Old Bill dashed to the mound checked me out again. He then went over to third base and got right up in his face. "Damn it Frankie, the kid just has a hell of a sinker today!" He bellowed for all to hear. "He ain't doctoring the ball. Now I'm going to tell you something, if you complain one more time, one more, I'm going to throw you out of the game and take some of your money!"

As Summer walked back to home plate, I turned to Frank and stuck my fingers in my mouth. Frank just turned around and groaned.

By the way, I never did throw the spitter. For one reason or another whenever I tried it, the pitch straightened out!

I recall another game we had with the Yankees in New York. It was an afternoon game and it became apparent that a few of the Yankees were hurting, especially Mickey Mantle, who looked tired or hurt. However, when he was hurting, he was as dangerous as a wounded bull. Mantle was a switch-hitter with power from both sides. I always thought he was a better highball hitter from the left side and a lowball hitter from the right side. I felt he had more power from the right side than the left, but he certainly didn't lack power from either side, and he could hit any pitch low or high out of the park, depending on the speed and location of the pitch.

In the first inning I got Mantle out on strikes. On the second time at bat, he hit a Texas leaguer to left center. I could tell by the way he ran he was hurting. When he came to the plate a few innings later, I called to him as I rubbed up a new baseball, "Hey, Mick!"

He responded, "What the hell do you want?"

I ran my hand back and forth under my chin, a knockdown sign, meaning I was going to give him a little chin music. He responded by giving me the drag bunt sign, meaning he would drop a bunt down the first base line and run up my back when I covered first.

My first pitch was a good fastball that sank low and away to the outside part of the plate. He had a great rip at the ball but missed it for strike one. I looked in again and gave him the chin sign once again. He just smiled and shook his head. I figured if he bunted and got a hit it would be better than him slamming one out of the ballpark.

I fired the next pitch and it was a little more inside than he thought it was and as he turned toward first to bunt the ball, he took a half swing as he tried to get out of the way and hit a solid line drive over second base. He was so strong.

When he returned to first I looked at him, shook my head and mumbled, "Spend some of that money on steaks that cheap food will kill you. That's two cheap hits in one game." We both laughed!

In 1959, we were playing a day game in Chicago against the White Sox. In the first inning, Luis Aparicio opened the inning with a walk then stole second base. Nellie Fox followed with a single to right to score Aparicio with the first run of the ballgame.

From that point on, I retired the next twenty-five White Sox hitters in a row. We took the lead, 2-1, in the top of the fifth on Faye Throneberry's two-run homer. That's the way the ball game stood, going into the bottom half of the ninth inning. The White Sox had the top of the batting order coming to bat in their half of the inning. Aparicio reached base on an error. Fox laid a perfect bunt down the third base line. Catcher Steve Korcheck anticipated the bunt and jumped on the ball like a cat. Steve had Nellie by ten feet at first, but he threw the ball into right field. Aparicio, who was off with the pitch, scored easily to tie the game at 2-2, Fox advanced to third when the cutoff man misplayed Throneberry's throw from right field. Now Fox was on third with no one out. The strategy for this situation was clear. Walk the next two hitters intentionally to fill the bases, bring the infield in to cut off the wining run and move the outfield in close so the runner on third could not score on a short ball to the outfield.

The White Sox brought in left-handed hitting Billy Goodman, a former teammate of mine at Boston and an American League batting champion, to hit for Jim Landis. With the count 2-2, Billy hit a normal fly ball to left field, deep enough to score the winning run. I walked off the field in a daze. How was it possible to lose such a perfectly pitched game? By the time I got to the clubhouse my German temper had kicked into gear and I was cussing, throwing my glove against the locker, literally ripping my uniform off my body. At that point in time, Boom-Boom Beck, who had been out in the bullpen in center field, entered the clubhouse. He approached me with compassion and tenderness, having experienced such disappointments himself as a pitcher. He tried to console me with words: "Dutch, you covered yourself with glory out there this afternoon!"

In reply, I turned on him like a pit bull! I called him everything that came into my mind. When I finally cooled off, I looked into his eyes and for the first time in my life, saw hurt in a fellow human being. At that moment I realized how much words could sting and hurt, and understood a lesson my father tried to teach me. Once words are spoken they can never be taken back. Boom Boom walked away. There was nothing more to say! I sank onto the chair in front of my locker, ashamed at my outburst, saddened with the loss, and concerned that I had lost a wonderful friend. At that point I must have felt a little like Peter felt when he denied Jesus three times.

Later that night I knocked on Beck's hotel room door. Tears rolled unashamed down my face as I begged him to forgive me for my outburst of anger. He took me by the shoulders and reassured me, "Dutch regardless of the outcome you covered yourself with glory out there this afternoon." I never forgot that feeling and I never let my temper control me again. Beck had taught me a valuable lesson.

There is more to learn in baseball than just playing the game. One skill I learned was art, and I'm not referring to the art of pitching. When I was with the Red Sox, I learned how to decorate balls, but it wasn't until I got to Washington that my new found hobby took off. I learned the skill from Del Wilber, who was a backup catcher with the Red Sox my rookie season. Del had a rather odd hobby that I immediately became interested in attempting. He would decorate baseballs using India ink and watercolor pencils. Several players on the team and others around the league would ask Del to decorate a ball when something occurred in their career that merited remembering, a grand slam home run, a low-hit shutout game, a record of one sort or another or any special game or feat that was accomplished. Del would draw cartoons and add a few words along with the inning-by-inning scores. I'd watch Wilber work and quickly picked up the method.

When Del was sold during the season, I began decorating the balls for special happenings, such as my first victory. I did a few other balls for close friends and it wasn't long before the guys began asking me to decorate a baseball for them. Jackie Jensen was one the first to ask. He hit his eighth grand slam home run and he wanted a ball to commemorate the home run. I was good at art as a schoolboy and that aptitude carried right into this hobby.

I finally got so many requests that the front office told me to stop and keep my mind on pitching. I continued to work the balls when we were at home and my time was my own and on long road trips when I hand time on my hands.

When I got traded to Washington, I continued the hobby. Two of the most remembered pieces of art

I took up the hobby of coloring balls when I wasn't busy pitching.

were done for Jim Busby and the Senator batboy, William Turner.

I never thought much about the decorated balls or what players said about my work until years after many of us had retired. I was asked in 1986 to attend a reunion of the last Washington Senators team to play in Washington. It marked the 35th anniversary of the move to Minneapolis by Clark Griffith. Twenty-five former Senators were in attendance including Busby. He approached me one evening and commented, "Russ, I never did get to thank you for doing those baseball for me. To tell the truth I have several golden glove and other awards, but those three ball are my families most popular possessions, and when I die they will most likely fight over who gets them."

Ironically, it was Busby who nearly allowed me the third home run in my career. We were playing a game at Fenway Park, and I hit a liner to left center. He went back to get the ball and caught it, but he crashed into the wall and knocked himself out. He fell on top of the ball and I ran all the bases for an inside-the-park homer, but the scorekeeper never gave me credit for the home run. He charged Busby with an error on the play.

Busby was the first of several players who, in the next several years, mentioned how important the balls were to their collection of baseball memorabilia. A few years later, I read where Jim passed away and I thought of what he had said that day.

Also during the anniversary, the batboy on the Senators team expressed his appreciation for the ball I did for him. "This is my most prized possession," said Turner. "Nobody, absolutely nobody, touches this ball without my permission."

I had sketched a small whale with a smiling face on one side, and out of the whale's spout came the words, "a whale of a batboy." Turner later sent me a letter saying, "What a great time I had at the 'Senator's Reunion.' It again revived my memories of all the wonderful times I had being a batboy for you guys. I am writing this letter while looking at a ball that is a treasure to me." He became the Sixth Judicial Circuit Judge in Maryland. How's that for doing something with your life after baseball? Isn't it strange that the people we meet as we work our way up the latter of life are the same people we meet on the way down the road of life? It's a good reminder to watch what you say and how you treat people.

The Senators were a unique group of men who were brought together by Calvin Griffith to bring respectability and interest to a team that had reputation of being the last place team in the American League. He was patient in his pursuit to find the brass ring. Most of the talent was in place before he was forced to move west. I feel sorry for the fantastic Senator fans that were not blessed to see the championship team bring the banner to Washington.

Calvin's search for talent was limited for three major reasons. First, teams were very reluctant to part with promising young minor league players. Secondly, he had to hold onto the talent he had and could not afford to gamble on an expensive trade or take a chance on the available veterans who demanded a higher salary. Finally, the Senators had a low budget and finishing last in the American League made the signing of talented young prospects extremely difficult.

Two distinct levels of ownership existed in baseball from its very beginning. The wealthy self-styled sportsmen considered baseball ownership more of a hobby than a profit-making business. The other level was made up of men or families that operated the team as a family business. The majority of owners were sportsmen. When Calvin became the president of the Washington Senator Baseball Club, he was probably confronted with more challenging situations than any other owner in baseball. He met these challenges with imagination, daring, and forceful, determined leadership.

Griffith Stadium was known as a pitcher's paradise. One of his first moves was to move the distant left field fence in closer to home plate giving hitters a better chance of reaching the seats. He also traded off such veteran favorites such as Mickey Vernon, Bob Porterfield (both to Boston Red Sox), and Mickey McDermott (to New York Yankees) for younger, fresher

Mickey Vernon

talent. Calvin totally revamped the ticket-selling system and for the first time promoted season ticket sales. He also introduced the sale of beer to the stadium. His acquisition of new players; an improved relationship between players and management, and a more exciting home run hitting team halted a 10-year attendance recession, and brought about a modest one-step rise in the league standings. These changes seemed to fore-shadow a better future for the Senators, but other major problems would prove more difficult to handle.

Griffith Stadium was one of the oldest stadiums in baseball, and the city fathers were reluctant to sink dollars into the old structure. The Redskins also used the stadium and the owners applied pressure to get the city to build a new facility for their premier football team.

Griffith was in favor of a joint facility, but arguments that developed over the parking and concessions rights hindered the progress of the discussion. Calvin was able to make expenses at the stadium, because the family owned and operated the concession stands and parking facilities, and the Redskins paid rent during the football season. Still, he found it increasingly difficult to manage a reasonable profit. His brothers, the Robertson twins operated the concession stands and parking facilities. His sister Thelma was a club executive and so was her husband, Joe Haynes, a former Senator pitcher. Calvin's brother, Sherry Robertson, a former Senator player, was the farm director. Without the profit from the conces-sions, parking, and rent from the Redskins, it would be impossible for the family to support itself. This became the hang-up that eventually led Calvin to make the decision to move the club to Minnesota in 1961. A family member told me, when the decision to move was finalized only $50,000 remained in the operating account.

Taking all these facts into consideration, it is easy to understand why Griffin was so tight fisted. For those of you who are old enough to remem-ber the buffalo on our five-cent coin, a story went around that Calvin was so tight-fisted that he squeezed the nickel so tight the buffalo defecated.

I personally believed that Calvin was fair in most circumstances — at least he was with me. The Senators had a difficult time scoring runs. Pitchers operated under the opinion that in order to win you had to throw a shutout and hit a home run. I was never considered a lucky pitcher. During a stretch of five games I started, I gave up a total of seven runs and fifteen base hits and never won a game. I lost three 1-0 games. Two of them were one-hitters, another was a 2-0 three-hitter, a 3-0 four-hitter and the final game was a 3-2 decision, which was lost in the ninth inning at Baltimore. I simply was not getting any offensive support. It's difficult to win when your team isn't scoring any runs.

When my contract arrived the next fall, I was certain that I would receive the same salary as the previous year. Much to my surprise I opened it to find a $3,000 raise. Needless to say, I signed and returned it the same day. I was afraid that they had made a mistake and I wanted it registered before they could change their minds. When I arrived at spring training, I took the time to personally thank Griffith for the raise. "You pitched well enough to win 20 games with a first-division club," he responded. "You deserve the raise."

In my opinion, Griffith was a true baseball man. He loved the game and he loved being around baseball people. By the time he left baseball, he was one of the last owners who understood the game from top to bottom. He took a great deal of heat from the fans, media, and people in general for moving the team out of Washington in 1960, but I believe he did what he felt he had to do to keep the family to-gether and at the same time stay financially viable. From purely a business standpoint, he really didn't have a choice. He had to go.

That's me in 1959.

My 1961 Topps card.

Chapter 7
The White Sox

E arly in the 1960 season, we were on a road trip to Detroit. The Senators were scheduled to play an afternoon game with the Tigers at Briggs Stadium. I had breakfast at the hotel with my roommate, Dick Hyde. Since it was a beautiful spring day and our hotel was just a short distance from the stadium, we decided to walk to the ballpark. The normal procedure on road trips was to get to the ballpark about three hours prior to game time. As we entered the visitor's dressing room, the clubhouse man told me that Cookie Lavagetto wanted to see me in his office. I reported and Cookie got right to the point. "Cal Griffith just called and told me you have been sold to the White Sox." The sum was undisclosed, but I didn't care what they got.

I don't recall saying anything, but I do remember a million thoughts racing through my mind, most of which were happy. I knew that Al Lopez and the White Sox had been trying to buy or trade for me for a couple of years, but I was surprised to learn it finally happened. The White Sox won the American League pennant in 1959 and had a great chance of winning it again. I was elated to be going from a team at the bottom of the standings to a first place-team, but I did have close friends on the Senators, and moving from one team to another always presents concerns, especially for the wife and children. I was simply taking my clothes and baseball gear to Chicago, where my major concern was to adapt to my new team and take advantage of playing with a pennant contender.

My wife Betty, on the other hand, faced the formidable task of informing our three children — Rusty, Cheryl, and Darrel — that their father was no longer with the Washington Senators, but the Chicago White Sox and most likely wouldn't be home again until the White Sox came to Washington or we drove up to Chicago.

Whenever a player was sold or traded, he had three days, according to the contract, to join his new club. I said my goodbyes to my friends and teammates, accepted their good wishes, packed my baseball gear, and headed to the hotel. I called home to tell my wife about the move to Chicago. We decided that the best thing to do under the circumstances was for me to go to Chicago, get settled, and see what was available there before we made any decisions. After the call, I packed my clothes, and caught a cab to the airport. I had time to daydream of what it would be like pitching for a winning team with great defenses for the first time in my pro career.

What the White Sox needed was a long right-handed relief pitcher and spot starter to add to their solid pitching staff. The Sox had Early Wynn, Billy Pierce, Bob Shaw, and Dick Donovan in the starting rotation. Frank Baumann and Herb Score were the long relievers, while Gerry Staley and Turk Lown were the closers.

They had also purchased Sievers from the Senators during the off-season. Roy had hit 102 home runs for Washington over the past three seasons; therefore, it appeared as if they had obtained the right-handed power hitter and RBI man needed to go along with Sherman Lollar, Minnie Minoso, Al Smith, and Ted Kluszewski. They would complement the middle of the order with line-drive hitters and speed men such as Luis

Aparicio, Nellie Fox, Jim Landis, Jim Rivera, and Gene Freese, to provide the run scoring possibilities the team lacked in its pennant drive the previous season.

The reserve players were solid replacements. Sammy Esposito, Billy Goodman, Earl Torgeson, Floyd Robinson, and the catching backups were Joe Ginsberg and Camilo Carreon.

The owner of the White Sox was Bill Veeck. He was born in Chicago and began his baseball career with his father, William, who was a sportswriter that ended up being president of the Chicago Cubs. He learned the business from the ground up working around the office, mailing out letters and working in the concession stands.

Veeck served with the Marines in the South Pacific during World War II and was injured when an anti-aircraft gun recoiled and shattered his foot, an injury that would lead to many operations and the eventual loss of his leg. He was a people person, who would rather sit in various sections of the bleachers during a game, visiting with the fans, than sitting in the comfort of the owner's box. He wanted a customer's view of the game. His promotional flair and antics brought him nothing but criticism, distrust, and censorship from the other owners, who thought his philosophy was a disgrace to the game. It didn't matter to him as the fans loved his style and his gimmicks drew massive crowds to the ballpark and set attendance records. He brought the exploding scoreboard to Comiskey Park the season I arrived there and every time a Sox player hit a homer, the thing would go off like the Fourth of July. Kids loved it. And nobody will ever forget Eddie Gaedel, the midget he sent up to bat when he was running the St. Louis Browns. His sincere loyalty to the fans along with his contagious enthusiasm propelled the 1959 "Go Sox" to the team's first pennant in 40 years.

From a player's point of view, Veeck was "The Man." He was never too busy to visit with the players or take time to listen to what they had to say. He treated everyone with the same attitude and respect, and often called the clubhouse after a game to congratulate players for outstanding performances. He held the respect of every player or employee whoever worked for him. His attitude was, "You don't work for me, but with me."

From the top of the lineup to the reserves, the White Sox had all the tools to repeat as American League champion. However, what made this team so very special was its compatibility. From the front office to manager Al Lopez through the coaching staff and down to the groundskeepers, the whole teams attitude and focus was one of harmony. Everyone just simply enjoyed being with one other, on and off the field. Talented, compatible, happy, relaxed, fun loving, and sociable might be a great summation of the team. I was never unhappy or dissatisfied with any of the four teams I played for during my career, but many of the best memories and lasting friendships occurred during my stay in Chicago.

I arrived at the White Sox locker room in Comiskey Park a few minutes before the end of batting practice. The clubhouse man barely had time to put my traveling bags in the storage room when the team made its way from the field to the locker room. I was greeted with far more enthusiasm than I expected. I certainly wasn't a stranger to most of the Sox players. I had been in the league for a few years and had battled the White Sox in several classic games in previous seasons, but I was not prepared for the welcome I received.

After a meeting with Lopez and the coaching staff, I was told that I would be in the bullpen for the game that evening and not to be surprised if I was called on to pitch. I found the clubhouse man and asked him to get me set up with a locker. The clubhouse was open in the center with lockers stationed along the outside walls. As I waited for the clubhouse man to get me a uniform, I stood in the center of the room. Most of the team sat in their lockers sipping a soft drink or changing undershirts for the game. Aparicio, Rivera, and Esposito approached me and began to walk in circles around me, muttering questions to each other. "What do you think? Seven, no maybe a six? Could be an eight?"

I wondered what they were doing? I eventually found out that they were evaluating the quality of the way I dressed and the area of the locker I was about to receive was dependent upon that evaluation. I was finally given a locker with Smith on my right side and Minoso on my left. I never did find out if my evaluation was good or bad, but I did pick up on the nickname — Oreo — because I was a white guy dressing between two black guys.

Whenever we experience a change in our lifestyle, whether it is forced upon us or is of our choosing, there is a period of adapting that takes place. Sometimes the transition is easy, sometimes it is dragged out. One of the good things about my trade to the White Sox was the immediate acceptance of the team and management.

I had already been told that I would be used in relief, so that first game with the White Sox came easy. After infield practice, I headed to the centerfield bullpen. Pierce started against the Red Sox and held a 4-1 lead going into the top of the sixth inning, but after getting Vic Wertz to fly to right for the first out he ran into trouble when Runnels singled to center, Don Buddin reached on a walk, and Willie Tasby hit a Texas leaguer just beyond the reach of Minoso and Smith to load the bases. With right-hand hitters Lou Hinton and Frank Malzone scheduled to hit, Lopez decided to go to his bullpen for help. I had been warming up along with Herb Score, but the situation called for a right-hander and sure enough I was called into the game to face my former teammates.

After making the lineup changes with the umpire at home plate, Lopez came to the mound, handed me the ball. "This is what we got you for," he said. "Now get us out of this jam!"

I was pumped up. My fastball was blazing, and I couldn't have been more excited. Hinton liked the ball up and away. I wanted to keep it down in the strike zone to force a ground ball that could be turned into a double play. On the first pitch — a slider — Lou was late and fouled it off. The second pitch was a flaming fastball that caught him looking. Lollar called for a fastball low and away, and it nicked the outside corner for strike three. Malzone stepped to the plate with two outs and the bases loaded. With the count two and two, he grounded to Fox at second, and we were out of the inning. I retired Boston on two hits the rest of the way to give Pierce a victory and me a save. Lopez was pleased. I was thrilled. The team was overjoyed.

After accepting the congratulations from my new teammates, Lopez called me into his office and told me that Veeck wanted to see me.

Veeck simply said, "Nice job, we have been trying to get you for sometime because we thought you could help us out just like you did tonight. Great start! Keep it up! By the way, I'll send down directions to my tailor's shop. Go get yourself a couple of custom-made suits. Nice game!"

I later learned it was just an example of how Veeck made a player feel at home. In my opinion, he was the best owner in baseball at the time. I might also add that from the moment I stepped into the clubhouse, I was an accepted member of the White Sox, and I never felt any other way.

If I had to choose one team that I enjoyed more than the others it would be the White Sox. Why the White Sox? Well, more than anything else, it was the make-up of the team. Some teams have the rah-rah guys who are always tense and upset when a little adversity comes their way. It's contagious and pretty soon the whole club is uptight and to play this game a level approach that uses the pressure in a positive way and at the same time allows you to relax and perform out of habit, not frustration. It's like driving a car. When you first learn to drive you review the steps. Put the key in the ignition, let out the clutch, ease down on the gas, look both ways, then put the car into motion. By the time you've driven for a few months, you do all these steps without thinking each one through. If a hitter has to stop and think of each movement of his swing most likely he'll take three pitches down the middle and never take the bat off his shoulder.

Most teams have a combination of players — some tight, some loose, and those who are neither. The White Sox were loose! I don't mean careless or not serious; they were able to play the game using their natural instincts and enjoyed the game. I don't mean to imply that we weren't upset with a loss, or a 0-for-4 day at the plate, or getting beat in a close game. It was simply having the philosophy that the baseball season is a marathon not a sprint and it takes the efforts and contribution of 25 players to run the course and claim the prize.

Being able to laugh at someone when they pulled a bone-head play was acceptable. Like the time we were playing the Yankees at home. The score was 2-2 going into the bottom of the seventh. Rivera singled and was advanced to second on a sacrifice bunt. Johnny Coats was on the mound for the Yankees. He had what might be called a long, slow delivery. Jim was positive he could steal third base and put us in a position to score the wining run on a fly ball to the outfield. Rivera watched Coates for a couple of pitches until he felt he knew just when to break for third. Yankee catcher Elston Howard must have picked up something from Jim, because no one flashed the steal sign. He called for a pitch out, and Coats used a short delivery to the plate. Rivera broke just as the ball headed for home. Howard received the pitch high and away from the hitter and threw Jim out at third by three feet. Everyone on the team moved to the far end of the bench away from Lopez and the other coaches because we knew a chewing out was in order. Rivera entered the dugout and sat on the very end of the bench away from Lopez. In a short time, coach John Cooney moved slowly toward Rivera. "The Senor wants to see you."

Everyone on the bench kind of snickered. Rivera had this sick look on his face as he slowly moved to a seat on the bench next to Lopez. Al glared at him for a moment then said, "What the hell were you trying to do?"

Jim hesitated, then replied, "Well, I thought..." That's as far as he got.

"Thought! You thought! You're not suppose to think. Thinking is my job. You just do what you're told to do and I'll do the thinking."

Jim never lived it down. In fact, we still tease him about it today about it.

Baseball has always had its bazaar moments and happenings on or off the diamond that stirred the fans imagination, such as Babe Ruth pointing to the centerfield bleachers and hitting a home run in the very location on the next pitch. Another was Eddie Waitkus being shot by a deranged female in the hotel. Most stories of this nature were not made public as much in my generation as they are now, but they happened just the same.

Bob Shaw was a good pitcher with the White Sox during their pennant winning season of 1959. He was also good looking, single and much sought after by the ladies. Jack Brickhouse covered the White Sox games for WGN-TV. He also had an attractive Oriental housekeeper. Shaw and I lived at the Del Prodo Hotel on the south side of Chicago and we took turns driving to Comiskey Park. One day Brickhouse approached Shaw as we were about to leave the parking area. "Hey Bob, I got a question for you. Are you dating an Oriental women?"

Bob smiled and replied, "No Jack, I'm not dating an Oriental woman."

"Oh come on." Jack said. " I know all about it, she's my housekeeper."

"You got the wrong guy."

A few days later Jack approached Bob again. "Shaw, what are you trying to hide? I checked with my housekeeper and she definitely said she's dating you."

"No, I'm not!" Bob insisted.

Brickhouse continued, "She says you come over to the house every day after a home game and you have your spikes, hat and glove with you."

"Why in hell would I do that Jack? My shoes, hat and spikes stay in my locker. When did you ever see a player take his equipment home with him every night?"

Brickhouse did not respond, but you could see the question marks flash in his eyes. The next day he came to the clubhouse prior to the game and suggested to Shaw that he believed someone was impersonating him and he had better have it checked out quickly. Brickhouse set up the arrangements with the police to take the guy into custody once the house-keeper had let him into the house. As a result, the fellow, who slightly resembled Shaw, was arrested for impersonating him. He was taking advantage of his look-a-like features and knowledge of White Sox base-ball to make advances to the ladies.

When I joined the White Sox, I soon realized the infield was designed with just the right amount of tilt toward the mound that prohibited the ball from rolling into foul territory. The reason for the tilt was Nellie Fox. If Nellie laid down a bunt within a foot or so of the doctored spot, he had a base hit. Let me assure you any protest from the visiting teams, directed toward the men in blue, fell on deaf ears. I don't want to make this sound like a devious practice, because every team took advantage of their assets. If a team possessed speed, the infield grass was cut a little higher, and shorter if your guys were slow of foot. The same was true of the outfield grass. Needless to say, the change from grass to Astro-Turf took away any of the advantages. When I was with the Senators, Washington moved the left field fence in to take advantage of the added right-handed power in their lineup. Other clubs made similar adjustments that would give the home team a possible edge.

The most notable difference between pitching for the Senators and the White Sox was defense. I was a low, sinking fastball pitcher that usually resulted in a high percentage of ground balls being hit when I pitched. All pitchers have a kind of built in sense that detects the destination of the batted ball the moment it is hit. When a batter really gets into a pitch you don't even have to follow the flight of the ball to know it's in the seats. Ground balls are immediately tagged outs or hits depending upon the solidness and direction of the hit. Most often our first instinct, hit or out is correct, however, players making great plays, being in front of a line drive and, the wind changing the flight of the ball cause us to be wrong at times.

It took me several games for my instincts to readjust to the Chicago defense, especially with Aparicio and Fox at short and second, respec-tively. Landis, Rivera, and Minoso in the outfield were terrific. Landis was one of those string-bean players, a little over six foot, who could float after the ball like Joe DiMaggio, who was noted for his ability to glide after the ball and somehow be there.

Landis saved many games for the Sox with his speed and instincts. Likewise, Minoso had the speed and desire to get anything hit in his direction. Rivera was special! "Jungle Jim" could go after it with the best. He would dive to make the catch, leap into the stands, or push beyond reason in an attempt to rob a hitter of extra bases. He simply did not understand anything less than 110 percent.

The defense turned so many hits into outs with spectacular plays it was a joy watching them perform day after day. I can't tell you how many times Aparicio or Fox would chase down a ball hit directly over second and flip it to the other infielder who would throw the runner out at first. The team's defense was almost taken for granted. I felt like a quarterback in the National Football League, who is protected from being sacked game after game by his offensive line. You learn to appreciate the skill and dedication of those around you.

As talented as any team may be, it can falter without leadership. The White Sox had that leadership on the field in Lopez. His teams topped the Yankees for the American League pennant in 1954 with Cleveland and again in 1959 with the White Sox. Al was quiet by nature but outspoken when it came to emphasizing his expectations of every player on the team. He was friendly toward his players and respected us. Handling the pitching staff and keeping twenty-five ego-hyped men content is the single most important area of the game for managers to understand.

Lopez also had a great group of coaches that he had handpicked to help him lead the team. His pitching coach, Ray Berres, had tipped him off to the difficulty with my sidearm delivery. Beres was great on teaching the fundamentals of pitching and throwing the ball. Other coaches on his staff were Tony Cuccinello, Don Gutteridge, and Cooney. They had a ton of experience to lend me and my teammates. Lopez's leadership can best be described as directed, no nonsense, and fair. Lopez calculated every move based on his intimate knowledge of the game and the men who played for him and against him. He recognized the various abilities of his player and used those talents to the best fit into the needs of the team. He exhibited fairness in his treatment of players.

From the top of the lineup to the reserves, the White Sox had all the tools to repeat as American League champions. However, we faded badly near the end of the 1960 season. Baltimore and New York held the hot hand. We lost seven or eight games in a row at one stretch and suddenly found ourselves dropping into third place behind the Orioles, which is where we finished the season 10 games behind the Yankees. While my first year with the White Sox was great — 6-3 record with a 2.98 ERA — it wasn't so great for the team, which finished in third place behind the Yankees and Orioles. I had hoped to get more starts with the White Sox, but it was not meant to be.

When the season ended, we sold our home in Alexandria, Virginia and moved to Bloomington, Illinois, a two-hour drive from Chicago. We moved to Bloomington because we had close friends there. Jim Bowers was my catcher when we played semi-pro baseball in Pittsburgh. He had a good chance of making it in the pros, but he was drafted into the Army and when he was discharged he decided to complete his college degree. Then he married a woman named Shingles and settled into coaching.

As it turned out, the decision to move to Bloomington proved to be great decision. We ended up living there for several years. During the off season, I had a nightly radio sports show, did the play-by-play of high school and college football and basketball games, and worked in public relations for the White Sox.

I also became close friends with Dr. Merill Smith, the pastor of our church, who was instrumental in my decision to enter into the ministry, which was one of the most important decisions of my life. Dr. Smith convinced me to study for the ministry. I worked with youth, visited nursing homes and shut-ins on Sunday. Then I began to take a few theo-logical courses at Wesleyan University.

In February 1961, I headed to spring training in Sarasota with great porspects of having a better year in 1961. The White Sox were not happy with the third-place finish in 1960 and went to work in the off-season to add pitching strength and depth to their staff. They picked up Juan Pizarro from Milwaukee, Ray Herbert from Detroit, Cal McLish from Cleveland, and Don Larsen from the Yankees. Shaw was traded to Kansas City. Baumann and I would sometimes start a game when need be.

In fact, I got only two starts during the season. The first came on June 4th and I beat the Yankees 4-2. I managed to give up a solo home run — number fifteen on the season — to Roger Maris, who was on his way to breaking Babe Ruth's record of 60 dingers in a season. I also gave up home-run number thirty-nine to Maris later in the season in New York. In the win over the Yankees, I pitched seven innings before Turk Lown came in to pick up the save. A week later on June 11, I shutout Kansas City on three hits for my second shutout of my career. In all, I made forty-seven appearances that season, winning three and losing three whith an ERA of 4.36. Hardly the number I expected or wanted, but that was a lot of outings in those days. The season record for number of appearances was sixty-five. For some reason the team never jelled that season and we ended up finishing in fourth place.

After the 1961 season, I went back to doing things in Bloomington, including my radio broadcasting. The first week in February, I was leaving the radio station one snowy day when I slipped on the stairs and went head over heels down several steps. I twisted my ankle so badly that I couldn't walk. The station owner took me to the emergency room and x-rays indicated no break, but it was severly sprained. Due to the nasty weather, I stayed off my feet and tried to help heal it by alternating hot and cold compresses. The treatment helped some, but when it became time to head to spring training I could hardly walk without crutches.

Lopez was not happy when I reported to spring training, because I was not able to participate in drills. Two weeks passed before I was able to trot. Not until the third week of camp was I able to throw to hitters. My name was at the top of Lopez's shit list. I was used sparingly the first couple of weeks, but thanks to the difficulties of the White Sox staff, I finally made a few appearances. Being on Lopez's list finally resulted in me being traded in June.

RUSS KEMMERER, Chcicago White Sox

Here's a publicity photo that had a glaring mistake in it.

This photo was taken at Wrigley Field when I first came to Houston.

My 1963 Topps card.

Chapter 8
The Colt 45s

On June 25, 1962, I was traded to the Houston Colts of the National League for Dean Stone. Ironically, it was the second time I had been dealt for the left-handed pitcher. The first time was when I was back when I was with Boston. Also, for the second time in my career I was uncertain of my future in baseball. Houston was one of two new expansion teams that entered into the league that season. The other team was the New York Mets.

The move to Houston did not hold a great deal of promise for extending my baseball career. Veteran players were brought in to keep the club respectable while the young prospects developed in the farm system. General manager Paul Richards was one of the best minds in baseball, and

93

I knew that he had tried several times to trade for me when he was at Baltimore.

Richards assured me that the organization believed I had the strength, knowledge, and experience to become a standout relief pitcher with Houston. I never felt negative about my future with the Colts because my faith encouraged me to trust in the Lord and He will direct my path. I always see the glass as half full rather than half empty. I look for the good and believe for the best. I can only see the present. Only God can see the future. One good thing about going to Houston was being in the National League and I would get to play in my hometown of Pittsburgh and give my family and friends a chance to see me play.

Houston played their games in a temporary facility called Colt Stadium until the Astrodome could be built. Playing under the blazing Houston sun and brutal humidity was close to being ridiculous, to say nothing of the crow-size mosquitoes that buzzed around like dive- bombers from a war zone. A story circulated around about the two mosquitoes that landed in the dugout. One mosquito said to the other while sizing up the menu for dinner. "Shall we eat him here or carry him away?" The other replied. We better hurry and eat him here or the big guys will get him!"

The main job at hand for the Houston organization was to field the best team possible, be respectable, and sign talented prospects that would lead the team to respectability before the fans became disgruntled. During the clubs first two years there were sixty-five players listed on the roster.

Four men were chiefly responsible for bringing Major League Baseball to Houston. George Kirksey and Craig Cullinan began the early efforts to lure an existing team to Houston. These two were joined by R.E. "Bob" Smith, an oil man and real estate magnate who was brought in for his financial resources, and Judge Roy Hofheinz, a former mayor of Houston and Harris County judge who was brought in for his salesmanship and political influence. Time after time their attempts to move an existing franchise to the city were rebuffed by the powers of the game. Rather than backing down they contacted several other would-be owners from other cities, and announced plans to start the Continental League to compete with the National and American League. This pressure and their interest in protecting markets in what was considered their major league prospective cities, forced baseball to add two teams to each league. Hofheinz assured the other owners that a domed stadium would eliminate the sweltering

Houston summers. The Colts were the first major league team permitted to play Sunday night games. The exemption was granted because the heat from noon to six o'clock was unbearable for both players and fans.

The city held a "Name the Team," contest and Colt 45's was selected along with team colors of navy blue and orange. The first team was a collection of cast-offs stocked primarily through an expansion draft held after the 1961 season. Harry Craft was the first Colt manager. The first major league season began on April 10, 1962. The Colts hosted the Chicago Cubs. Veteran pitcher Bobby Shantz pitched a complete game and claimed an 11-2 victory for the Colts first major league win. Bob Aspromonte, a former teammate of mine with the Red Sox claimed a place in Houston baseball history by getting the first hit and scoring the first run. Roman Mejias hit the first two home runs and was the hitting star of the game. The Colts went on to sweep the three-game series from the Cubs and ended up tied for first place. But soon after finishing their first road trip, they learned a valuable lesson. The Major League Baseball season is a marathon and not a sprint. A one-hundred sixty-two game schedule brings the cream to the top.

The minds that make the decisions decided to add a little flare to the team when we traveled. Each player was fitted for a tailor-made, western styled, royal blue suit, complete with a Navy ten-gallon hat and blue Texas boots with orange trim, a white-and-blue pin-stripped shirt, and a orange tie. Needless to say, it was mandatory to wear the outfit whenever we were traveling with the team. I can't remember the number of times we were asked if we were part of a rodeo. Collectively, we thanked God that most of our flights were chartered. When it came to team unity, we were all in accord. The first thing we did after we checked into the hotel was to take off the outfit, hang it in the closet, and forget about it until we left town.

One of the great human-interest stories of that season revolved around Bob Aspromonte. Bob had befriended a young Arkansas boy who was struck by lightening while participating in a baseball game. When Bob visited the nine-year old at Methodist Hospital, the kid asked his hero to hit a home run for him that night. The infielder wasn't known for his long ball power, but he promised to do his best. As fate provided, Aspromonte blasted a homer. The following season the boy returned to Houston for additional eye surgery. Bob visited the kid again and once more was asked to hit another home run. This time he hit a grand slam to beat the Cubs, 6-

95

2. The press and the team latched onto the story that had gained league interest. When the boy came back to town in July he asked Bob for yet another home run. Aspromonte was stuck in a terrible slump and didn't want to disappoint the boy. Instead, he beat the Mets with another grand slam. If I had anything to do with it, I would have made the kid our batboy for the rest of the season.

Besides my pitching experience, I also brought my musical background to the team. I told coach bobby Bragan about my experience with the Singing Senators and it wasn't long before we were singing in the shower and had gained the interest of a few teammates: Jim Umbright, Hal Smith, and coach Cot Deal. We met the Buffalo Bills, who were so popular in the movie *Music Man*, in St. Louis and became friends with the group made up of Jim Jones, Scotty Ward, Vern Reed, and Hershel Smith. We made arrangements to see them twice more during the summer when our schedules coincided with their summer stock schedule. As the year progressed, we sounded pretty good. Late in the season, the Buffalo Bills, were scheduled to be on the Arthur Godfrey radio show in New York City. I remember us getting into town and having just enough time to get to the hotel, shed those blue cowboy suits and get to the studio. Our plan was simply to listen to them perform for the show. Godfrey lived on his farm in Virginia. He would fly into New York on Monday, tape the shows for the next week and return home. The five of us waited as Godfrey and the Bills taped the first session. When they took a break, Arthur asked Jim Jones who we were. He explained our friendship and our interest in music, and introduced us to Arthur. Godfrey said he wanted to hear us sing, so we returned to the studio and sang a couple of numbers. He thought we were really good and made the decision to redo the program they had taped. As a result we appeared on the Godrey show with the Buffalo Bills for the whole week.

By the end of the 1962 season, it was apparent that management made the decision to drop the veteran players and move with the future of the team. Staying with the veterans would result in a losing season. Bringing up the young players would also result in a losing season but provide the youngsters with valuable experience. Jim Wynn, Rusty Staub, Ken Johnson, Johnny Bateman, and Bob Bruce moved into the starting lineups and the older players took the reserve roll.

Personally, I had mixed emotions about my season. I was called on in

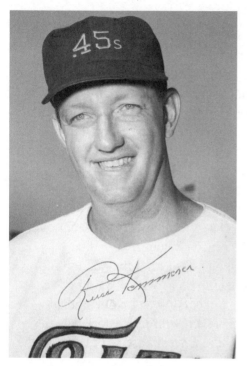

36 games with two starts and 34 relief appearances. I won five, lost three with an ERA of 4.10. I had moved to a relief roll with the White Sox, but had hoped to regain a starting slot with the Colts, but that never happened. I did have a couple of unique moments that year. I pitched in 13 consecutive games in relief. I should explain that although the games were consecutive, there were off days and a couple of rained out games that separated them. One big thrill was coming into a game in the ninth inning with the bases loaded and one out. My first pitch to Atlanta infielder Milt Bowling was a sinking fastball that he grounded to short for a double play. Following an off day the St. Louis Cardinals came into town. Once again I entered the game with the bases loaded and one out. Stan Musial was called on to pinch hit for the right- handed Cardinal hitter. I started "Stan the Man," one of my boyhood idols, out with a sinking fastball that he grounded to second for an inning ending double play. In two games, I recorded four outs on two pitches. Later in the season we were playing a day-night doubleheader with the Mets in New York. I came into the game in the late innings with the score tied. We scored one run to take the lead, and I shut down the Mets the rest of the way to gain the victory. In the second game that night I entered the game in the eighth with the score tied again. I held the Mets scoreless for two innings and we scored one in the ninth to win for the second time that day. I never checked the records but two wins in one day must at least tie a record.

Mejias was the team's leading hitter with a batting average of .286 with 24 home runs, 76 runs batted in, and twelve stolen bases. Dick "Turk" Farrell was the team's leading pitcher with 10 wins and 20 losses. He was the teams first All-Star selection, and played in both All-Star games played that year.

At the end of the season, every Houston player was given a complete physical examination. Umbright, my roommate, a classy pitcher, and wonderful competitor, was picked up from the Pittsburgh Pirates. Jim had a great deal of promise and had a winning record in his first two seasons with the Colts. During the examination a tumor was discovered in Jim's right leg turned out to be malignant and surgery was performed during the off- season. He rejoined the club at spring training in 1963, but returned to Houston prior to the season opener. He passed away before opening day. Jim's family asked me to conduct the services. It was one of the most difficult things I ever had to do. Ten thousand people attended the ceremony and local TV stations covered the service. Jim's death hung over the team like a black cloud as the 1963 season began.

At the start of spring training in Arizona, I was not included in the clubs plans for the season. Just after opening day I was asked to go to Oklahoma City to work with the young pitchers on technique and specialty pitches. Grady Hatton, who I had played with in Boston, was the manager. Grady was great to work with and a great baseball man with the personality to motivate the younger players. The kids developed quickly and midway through the season, we found ourselves involved in a tight race for the Eastern division of the Pacific Coast League. I suddenly began to have serious thoughts about a career as a pitching coach.

Houston was struggling to find some respectability and the powers to be made the decision to call up a couple of the more successful youngsters from Oklahoma City in hopes that they would encourage the Houston fans to acknowledge the future promise of the Colts. Grady and I were both against the moving of the young pitchers because neither of us felt they were ready to challenge major league hitters. Throwing them up against the power hitters of the National League could have a negative reaction on them and undo everything that had been accomplished in Oklahoma City. We felt we had a real chance of winning the Pacific Coast League championship and argued that winning the top minor league title would do more good for the organization and the Houston fans than the appearance of two pitching prospects. Besides, they could have their cake and eat it too. If we won the title and the kids had a major part in the victory, management in Houston would have the better of two worlds. Our plea fell on deft ears, and the pitchers were called up. The decision would make it very difficult for us to win our division of the league, but all we could do was hope someone else would take up the slack and we would still come out on top. Grady and I usually drove to the ballpark together and of course our conversation centered on the pitching rotation and who might best fill the void "Russ, I'll tell you who is going to stand in the gap and fill the void-you are going to be the man! I put you back on the active roster this morning. The Colts don't feel they have anybody ready to move up in the system and they want to win this championship if at all possible."

Strange things happen in this life there I was all setting myself up to be a pitching coach and suddenly I was called upon to set an example for the kids I have been coaching all season. I wasn't concerned about my arm or throwing well enough to win, but I did think of how embarrassed I would be if I didn't pitch well enough to prove my pitching theory was sound. I didn't need to worry I won six starts in a row, three of them shutouts, and we won our division, by three games over Dallas. We looked forward to taking on the top Dodger farm club from Spokane, Washington, winners of the western division, in the Junior World Series.

The series was set up to play three games in one city and the remaining games, of the best of seven series, in the other city. Since Spokane had the best winning percentage in the league the first three games were played in their ballpark. They jumped on us big time! I lost the first game three to one. We got pounded in the next two games and it appeared we were going to have a short series. We returned to Oklahoma City to try to extend the series beyond four games. Dave Giusti shut them down four to one to register our first victory and set the series totals at three games to one. We jumped out quickly in the fifth game behind the pitching of veteran Ben Johnson and won it going away nine to two. I threw one of the best games of my career in winning the sixth game of the series 9-0. I only threw 87 pitches and was in complete command the whole game. In the seventh and deciding game, Giusti shut them out, 4-0. We accomplished the impossible by coming back from a three games down to win the Junior World Series four games to three. Houston was happy, Oklahoma City was happy, I was happy and Grady Hatton was on cloud nine.

A few days later, when the celebration finally ended in Oklahoma City, Grady told me that one of the big brass in the Colt's front office had assured him of the manager's job for next season. He wanted me to go with him as his pitching coach. He said that Richards, the general manager of the Colts, was impressed with the job he had done managing at Oklahoma City, and the developing of the young pitchers that had taken place under my coaching.

Until this time, I had not given serious thought to continuing my baseball career as a coach. But now, considering what Hatton told me, I felt there was a good possibility of coaching at the major league level. I had gained a great deal of confidence watching the progress made by the young pitchers, and this altered my thinking. After much prayer and thought about my future and what was best for my family, we agreed to take the offer if it was presented.

It just never happened! Evidently, it was one of those promises made by someone in the Houston front office in the heat of passion then put aside once the total picture of the organization was considered.

Lum Harris was appointed as the new manager replacing Craft late in the 1964 season. Harris had big-league managing and coaching experience with the Braves. Hatton had big league playing experience, but no managerial experience, except for one season at Oklahoma City. Grady ended up taking a job in the Houston front office. He told me he tried to persuade Harris to give me the coaching job, but coaching position in baseball are most often passed on to former teammates and friends with some coaching experience, and not handed out to anyone who was not part of the system. It was clear to me if they really wanted to consider my ability to coach pitchers I would have been offered a job coaching at some level in the organization. I was 33 years old and by all standards it was evident that my professional baseball career was over.

Chapter 9
Then & Now

Before baseball was ever a business, it was a game. The invention of the game was first attributed to a West Point cadet by the name of Abner Doubleday. American baseball developed out of bat and ball games, such as rounders, town ball, and the English game of cricket. In 1845, Alexander Cartwright, a member of the New York Knickerbockers Club, published a version of what is now considered to be the foundation of the game. It called for bases ninety-feet apart, a diamond-shaped infield, a forty-five foot pitching distance, and a nine-man team. A number of different varieties were tried from time to time, but this version of the game caught on and replaced all of the competing forms.

In 1847, a group of sportsmen in New York, crossed over the Hudson

River to Elysian Fields, laid out a diamond, agreed upon rules, and played a game we call baseball. It began as a gentlemen's sport, and like everything else in this changing industrial society, it came with a rush and took the country by storm. Names such as John Montgomery Ward and Albert Spalding were associated with forming teams and playing the game. One might compare the growth of golf in our society today with the popularity of baseball in the late 1800. Throughout the years there have been many modifications, which tend to remind us that baseball is a constantly evolving sport.

I believe it would be a fair assumption to say that in the 100 years from 1845 to 1945, there were significant changes that took place in the game. It would also be safe to say that the majority of these changes had to do with rule and equipment changes, the regulations on bat size and ball size, and the introduction of night baseball and numerous others that altered the course of the game. It is not my intention to elaborate on each of these changes, however; I do want to point out what I consider to be major differences in baseball of the 1940s-1960s, and the game of baseball today.

Baseball following World War II and on through the sixties, is often referred to as the golden era of the American game. More players were elected into baseball's Hall of Fame during that era any other period of its history. Baseball in post-war America was truly the Great American Pastime. Many of its greatest stars, such as Ted Williams, Joe Coleman, Bob Feller, and a host of others returned from serving their country to the game they loved. The country needed to cast off the war cloud that hung over this country and the world, and baseball proved to be the answer! It was a time in our history when *Take Me Out To The Ballgame* really meant something. Baseball became a family sport with Knot-Hole Days, Ladies Day, and Sunday double-headers. Dad could take the family to the ballpark for a few bucks and Sunday dinner was a couple of hot dogs, popcorn, and a soda. Players were more or less fixtures on teams. The hometown heroes were more accessible to the fans and loyal to the city and team. They became the game's best salesmen.

The radio broadcast and newspaper reports of the games were the main methods of keeping tabs on your favorite team and players. When television arrived in the late 1940's, it was an expensive novelty not available to the majority of fans; therefore, the radio broadcast and sport columns continued to provide the lighthouse of baseball information. It was common to walk through the neighborhood on a warm summer night and hear a dozen radios blaring the play-by-play description of the game. In many cases, the announcers were just as much heroes as the players. Fans would listen to the game on the car radio, sitting in the living room, walking in the park or on the loudspeaker at work.

Those of us who cherish those days with the Pittsburgh Pirates can never forget the thrill of listening as announcer "Rosie" Rosewell described the flight of a home run ball off the bat of Ralph Kiner, and hear the breaking glass as he bellowed, "Open the window Aunt Minnie, here she comes."

And who could ever forget the exuberant description of Bobby Thompson's home run in the playoff game between the Giants and Dodgers that won the pennant for the Giants, or the Southern drawl of Mel Allen the voice of the Yankees, or the electric excitement of Red Barber broadcasting the World Series.

Only eight teams competed in each league. There were no playoff games or wild card teams. The season was topped off with the World Series the first week in October instead of at the end of the month. But then, those were the days! You might consider what you have just read as an old ballplayers nostalgic memory, and reach a conclusion that I am suggesting a returning to the, "good old days." But that's not my intent, anymore than suggesting we do away with our fast cars and return to the horse and buggy or throw out our computers and televisions. Simply put, this is the way it was in baseball's golden days.

Because there were only eight teams in each league, we got to know each other pretty well. There weren't many secrets regarding baseball habits, such as where a hitter liked a pitch, or his bad habits, liking chasing bad pitches. We were a close-knit group, especially the pitchers. We were a fraternity. Pitchers around the league would share information on how they were getting hitters out. This was especially true of teams you had been with before because we maintained our friendships. It was not unusual to have dinner with a former teammate when on the road. Hitters did the same thing. They'd ask about pitchers and what they threw.

I would imagine that this same kind of thing happens today, but differently. Today's baseball information is computerized. The information is more complex, like how many times a player hits to right or left, or what pitch he swings at most often. And a whole lot more.

Many changes in baseball have occurred since my time, most of them for the good of the game. Astro-Turf speeded up the game. Better equipment like shoes and gloves led to more exciting defense. Better bats and tighter wound baseballs have resulted in more home runs, making the game more exciting for fans. Doing away with the old flannel uniforms and replacing them with lighter fabrics and more colorful combinations was a move in the right direction.

I have heard it suggested that players today are stronger than we were, but I have my reservations. Guys like Jimmy Foxx, Mickey Mantle, Willie Mays, Ralph Kiner, Walt Dropo, Luke Easter, and Harmon Killebrew were big and strong. We believed in strength training, but our programs came about by working on farms or in eight-hour shifts in a steel mill. Today, players lift weights, have personal trainers, and nutritious diets designed to keep them in top shape all year long. Every major league ballpark has a weight lifting and conditioning room as well as experts to oversee the proper use of the equipment.

One of the things that has changed drastically from the days I played and now are autographs. We were more receptive to the fans when I played and would honor autograph requests at no cost to the fan because it helped promote the sport and satisfy the fan seeking autographs. Nowadays, many players want some sort of compensation for their autograph. Some charge a lot money for their signature and some fans are gullible enough to pay for it. Even now when somebody sends me money for an autograph, I return the money and send them an autograph. Now if they want a photograph that's a different story, because it costs me to make copies of photos, so I will charge for that service. And they will have to pay to get a copy of this book. But for an autograph? No.

Our contracts prohibited us from taking part in any contact sport, such as football, basketball, hockey, and boxing. Lifting weights was certainly not allowed. One of the old wives tales of our day was that lifting weights would develop muscles that would make it impossible to throw a ball or swing a bat properly. The world of athletics had little information on the positive effects on proper physical training. Not long ago in a conversation I had with Whitey Herzog. "I believe today's players could be ready to play a game in three days after reporting to spring training, except for the pitchers who need about two weeks to get their arms in shape." He commented," In my days you came to spring training to get in shape. Now they come to sharpen their skills because they are already in shape.

One reason young pitchers were invited to spring training with the parent club in my days was to throw the majority of batting practice and take part in the early Grapefruit League games until the veterans were in shape. It was good experience for young players and gave us a taste of what playing in the big show was like. When the veterans were in shape they would ship us off to the minor league camps. No longer are pitchers used for batting practice and some will pitch in other leagues during the off-season, such as the Arizona League in the fall or the Caribbean Leagues during the winter.

I believe today's teams have better knowledge and understanding of the human body, how it works. They take more advantage of training and teaching methods, do more one-on-one, hands-on teaching, and get a great deal more medical advice regarding injuries than we ever dreamed existed in our day. Players in my day were reluctant to disclose an injury in fear of being sent immediately to the minor leagues. I don't mean to imply that injures were ignored or teams refused to look into injuries. It was easier to send a borderline player to the minor leagues, trade, sell, release or re-place him, than it was to treat an injury. If he recovered, he could be recalled. If the new player worked out, great; if not, another player would be given an opportunity to succeed. Nowadays, surgeons are performing minor miracles for some players and having them back on the playing field when in my days their career would be over.

For the most part, players of my generation learned by trial and error, or by working with another player on techniques, or how to throw a new pitch or hints on how to hit to the opposite field, or a new batting stance, or anything that would help his game. Again I am not implying that the coaching was inadequate in our day, but the majority of coaches were not hired to teach or coach in the same capacity of today's coaches. Bernie Allen described Billy Martin as one of the most knowledgeable managers and coaches he was ever around, and testifies to the fact that he learned more from Billy about playing the infield than anyone else in his career. He tells the story of the young rookie at spring training that made an error in a spring training game and as he entered the dugout Martin approached him. The kid expected some teaching comment, like "Stay down on the ball."

Instead Billy replied, "It's okay kid, don't worry about it. You don't belong in this league anyway." The type of minor and major league teaching today developed only after major league players retired and took jobs as college coaches. College baseball in those days, was a joke and not very well accepted by those in professional baseball, but now the college game is a major source of drafted players.

One example of a player's development resulting from teammates taking an interest in a young player was Killebrew. When I first saw Harmon at spring training with the Washington Senators, he couldn't even touch a good fastball up in the strike zone in batting practice. Roy Sievers and Jim Lemon went to work with Harmon, made adjustments in his stance and swing, and after a trip to the minor leagues he returned to the majors and eventually right smack into the Hall of Fame.

One thing has remained constant in baseball since the very start is the reserve clause. It was interesting to find that one of the first things the owners or organizers of the leagues discovered is that they needed to find a way to keep the better players from jumping to other teams or leagues. They settled upon an agreement that would allow each team to protect five players. The players were pleased with the idea of being the best five on each team and accepted the label as a point of pride, never realizing that it would prohibit them from going to another team for more money. The owners called it a gentlemen's agreement. In reality, it was the beginning of the reserve clause. The number of players covered later increased to eleven and eventually covered every player in the game.

Whenever the subject of the reserve clause is brought up, the name of Curt Flood, the great St. Louis Cardinal outfielder, is associated with the changes made in the clause that absolutely is the most significant change in baseball history. In 1969, the Cardinal's traded Flood to Philadelphia. He wanted to finish his career in St. Louis. He had been with the club since 1958, and he had strong ties in the city. He had an established a photographic and art business, and he was an outstanding portrait painter. He refused to accept the trade, quit, and filed a federal lawsuit against baseball, Commissioner Bowie Kuhn and the Cardinals, stating that he had a right to receive offers from clubs other than Philadelphia. Flood lost the case and his appeal. Books have been written about baseball's reserve clause, and the players fight for free agency. My goal is to provide the reader with a few graphic illustrations of the reserve clause and what affect it had on players in my generation.

When a player signed a contract with a professional baseball team, he became the out-right property of that team unless they sold or traded him to another team, and transferred the ownership rights, which is sort of like being a slave If a club wanted to release a player, as was my case with Houston, it was necessary to place him on the waiver list with the stipulation that his name was placed there for the sole purpose of giving the player his outright release and his name could not be withdrawn. Players were often placed on the waiver list as a means of testing the interest that he might generate on the market in order to stimulate a trade with the interested club. The owning club could withdraw a players name at any time. If they choose not to remove the name the player could be picked up by any team in the league for the lofty price of $1.00. Even if you were released by a team or quit they still owned you under the reserve clause.

In 1962, I was traded by the White Sox to the Houston Colts, one of two new expansion teams in the National League. The next year, my arm had not responded to treatment during the winter months, and Houston made the decision to place me on waivers for the purpose of giving me an outright release. Once I cleared waivers, they sold my contract to Oklahoma City and offered me a minor-league contract. This accomplished three things. It opened a place on the forty-man roster, allowed them to maintain the rights to my services, enabled them to reduce my major league contract from $20,000 to $6,000, and gave them the right to purchase my contract from Oklahoma City without notifying any other teams. The biggest problem this presented for me was losing my hospitalization and medical benefits by not being on a major league roster the first day of spring training.

My wife Betty had undergone cancer treatment the previous year and needed to continue treatments. I pleaded with the club to keep me on the Houston roster for a day or two after training opened. They had to deny my request because I had cleared waivers under the purpose to release clause, making it impossible to withdraw my name.

Clearing waivers gave me a clear-cut, flag waving signal — every club in baseball had passed on me. Signing a minor league contract would not provide any hospitalization benefits. The logical decision was to retire and take the offer from Indiana University to coach and finish my degree. Hospitalization would be provided by the Methodist Church in Indiana.

But it would be necessary to pay the hospital for any treatments provided since the end of the previous season.

A few years, later Jim McIntyre, a broadcaster at Louisville when I played there, was broadcasting radio and television games for the Indianapolis Indians, an American Association baseball team. He wanted me to do the color commentary for twenty televised games, and I accepted. Les Moss, who was a bullpen catcher when I was with the White Sox, was the manager of the Indians. One day, the Indians needed someone to throw extra batting practice to a couple of players who were in a slump. Les asked me if I wanted to give it a shot. I hadn't thrown a baseball in almost two years but I agreed to give it a try. I pitched about twenty minutes of batting practice and the arm felt real good and didn't hurt. Surprisingly I was throwing the ball well after being out of baseball for two years, so I continued to throw for the next month. As the season made its way into mid-June, Moss called me into his office prior to batting practice and his question surprised me, "Russ, who owns your contract"?

"Houston. What's up?" I replied.

"I don't know if you realize it or not but your throwing the ball as well now as you were when I saw you in Chicago," he responded. "The Sox are going to call up a couple of our pitchers and they want to sign you for the rest of the season. If things go well don't be surprised if they call you up in September when the roster opens up."

I was thrilled! The medical bills for Betty were piling up making things tight and the $10,000 the club was offering would sure help out. A few days later Les called me into his office again. "I'm sorry but Houston won't release you! They want two of Chicago's top prospects and they were not willing to make the deal."

I was stunned! I believed that when I was place on the waiver list with the intent to release clause I was free. They refused me the courtesy of leaving me on the major league roster for one week at spring training so I could maintain the medical insurance, and they offered me a contract for with a $12,000 pay cut. I had not heard from them in more than two years, and I had not received a contract offer from them during this period of time. Still, they owned me and would until the day I died. I had no right to negotiate a baseball contract for myself that could perhaps give me one more opportunity to play at the major league level.

I can assure you I certainly could sympathize with Flood and any other ballplayer who may have had this type of experience under the reserve clause. I had an opportunity to resume my career and was denied that opportunity. I could have filed a lawsuit, but I neither had the money or the time to drag it through the courts. Is it any wonder that every player who played the game, cheered when baseball players finally received some relief from the dreaded reserve clause? Most baseball fans knew of the reserve clause, but never understood exactly how it operated. I hope this will provide a little better insight into why the players were willing to go on strike to alter it. Far too many fans were angry because they believed that the strike in 1995 was about money. I guess in some ways it all boils down to money but there were other issues that had an impact on the negotiations.

One of the more significant changes in baseball was in the area of contracts. My generation of players never even thought about a multi-year contract, at least I never heard it mentioned. The Uniform Major League Contract was for one year. If any of the super stars, like Williams, Mantle or Musial, had agreements for more than one season most likely it was single-year deals post-dated and signed in advance. Actually, this is difficult for me to believe because of the data used to determine the payroll that affected each player's salary for the coming season. Teams would use total attendance, where the club finished in the standings, how ticket sale for the coming year were progressing, expected food sales and parking revenue. Then the players salaries were penciled in.

In 1941, Joe DiMaggio hit .357 with 30 home runs and 125 runs batted in. He also had the record of hitting in 56 straight games. Supposedly, the Yankees wanted to cut Joe's salary $5,000. He was holding out for a salary increase to $25,000, and the press, radio, and fans were upset that he would demand such a lofty salary for playing baseball when most people were worried about the war in Europe and having trouble finding a job.

In 1957, Roy Sievers led the American League with 42 home runs and 114 runs batted in, and hit .301 for the Washington Senators. When he received his contract for 1958, he was offered a $10,000 cut. The club had finished in last place in the league, attendance was down and fans were not knocking down the ticket window doors to purchase pre-season ticket. When Roy spoke with Cal Griffith about the contract, Cal responded, "Roy we finished in last place in spite of your hitting, and we can finish last without you. Sign the contract!" He finally signed for a $4,000 raise, which most likely was what Calvin wanted to sign him for in the first place. I really believe that neither owners nor players were making a lot of money in the post-war days.

One year, when Bill Veeck was the owner at Cleveland, he set a table outside his office and placed each players contract in an envelope so that they could look at the offer and accept or reject it. It is said that all but one of the players signed the first offer.

When Al Kaline hit .287 one year, so he told the Tigers, "I don't want a raise. I'll sign for the same thing as last year! Then I'm going to have a great year and really make you pay." We had no agents; there were no multi-year deals and certainly no large television contracts and no large amounts of extra monies that would drive up the salary scale.

A couple of other sections of the uniform contract I believe will give a clear picture of just how much control the owners had over the players. There is a section listed as 3 (a) Loyalty: "The player agrees to perform his services hereunder diligently and faithfully, to keep himself in first class condition and to obey the Clubs training rules, and pledges himself to the American public and to the Club to conform to high standards of personal conduct, fair play and good sportsmanship." I guess I'm not exactly sure what that means but when I think about it, probably the most serious problem existed in our day was players drinking too much of the sauce, and perhaps a bar fight or two. When you look at modern problems and athletes, the name of Darryl Strawberry leaps to the front. He has been convicted of numerous drugs violation, parole violation, solicitation and what else only he knows. I'm not trying to pick on him, actually I feel sorry for him. I feel sorry for anyone who has an opportunity to use his or her abilities for the good of mankind and tosses it away senselessly. He is not alone.

One more section that will grab you is c (3). The player agrees that his picture may be taken for still photographs, motion pictures or television at such times as the Club may designate and agrees that all rights in such pictures shall belong to the Club and may be used by the Club for public-ity purposes in any manner it desires. The player further agrees that during the playing season he will not make public appearances, participate in radio or television programs or permit his picture to be taken or write or sponsor newspaper or magazine articles or sponsor commercial products without the written consent of the club. I wonder how this would fit in with today's contracts and the players and agents?

The majority of my generation players were grossly inept at presenting our point of view as to why we deserved a contract increase. Agents today have a wealth of information at hand with just a click of the computer regarding teams, profits, other player's salaries, and more. We had nothing but our stats to argue for an increase. My rookie season I made the minimum major league salary, $5,000. I joined the team in late May. I pitched in various relief rolls until July 18th when I made my first start. I ended the season with 5 wins, 3 losses, and an earned run average of 3.84. I lost some close games but all in all I felt it was the kind of year that proved to Boston that I could pitch in the league. Contracts usually arrived in mid-December. As November moved toward December I began to speculate the amount of increase I would receive. I finally set my sights on a $2,000 raise. The minimum salary in the major leagues had been increased from $5,000 to $6,000. So in reality I was only hoping for a $1,000 increase. I was disappointed when I opened the contract and found that they were offering the base salary of $6,000. I returned the contract unsigned along with a letter to Joe Cronin explaining why I deserved and was requesting $7,000.

A few days later Joe called me and asked me one question, "Would you rather play in Louisville or Boston next year? Think about it and before you decide, remember you're part of the pension plan and you don't want to throw that out the window. Sign the contract or prepare to go to spring training with Louisville." He hung up before I had a chance to argue my points. A few days later the same contract calling for a salary of $6,000 arrived. I signed it and sent it back. I was well out of my league when it came to negotiations. That's why agents are so valuable to players today.

A few years ago, Wade Boggs was attempting to become the first non-pitcher to get a million in arbitration. Gene Ozra, a union attorney, didn't like the way things were going, so when it came time for the final arguments he stepped in for Bogg's agent. He began his summation as he picked up a copy of *The Baseball Encyclopedia*, and began. "There are 13,000 players in this book, everyone who has played in the major leagues since 1871. You will only find two players, Ty Cobb and Rogers Hornsby that have a higher batting average than Wayne Boggs. Take this fact into consideration before you make your decision." Boggs won his million dollar salary fight. Ozra simply overwhelmed the arbitration team. He was right except for one major fact, Hornsby and Cobb's average were recorded over 20 or more years in the major leagues. Boggs' average was acquired in only three. It's a little like comparing a full grown orange to a seed. All that I can say is I sure would have like Ozra arguing for me. I might just have gotten my $2,000 raise.

As I sit and ponder the past and the present in baseball and diligently attempt to keep things in the proper perspective, a few words of the Simon and Garfunkel song, *Mrs. Robinson,* flashed across my mind, "Where have you gone Joe DiMaggio?" I quickly reminded myself that baseball, like everything else in life changes and moves on. Man was not created to stand still; therefore, we need to look to the future of the game while at the same time giving credibility to its history. Which brings up these questions: Where is baseball headed, what are the major problems in today's game and what can baseball fan expect in the future?

Another major change that has taken place in baseball is the pension plan. In 1947, a plan to develop a pension, hospitalization, and medical benefits plan for major league baseball players, including a term insurance policy for $10,000, was agreed upon by the owners and players.

The plan called for players to contribute fifteen cents a day to the plan and the owners would pitch in with sixty cents. A player had to be in the majors, and a contributor in the plan for five years in order to be eligible for a pension at age 65. The amount that a player would receive in benefits would depend upon the total number of years he was in the plan before he retired. For example, if a player had 20 years in the plan he could draw $250 a month for life. If he had 10 years the amount drawn would be $125 a month for life. Some players, such as Cal Ripken and Ted Williams, played twenty years or more in the major leagues, but the average tenure of a major league player is seven years.

By the time I made it to the American League, the plan had been refined. The players in 1953 contributed $3 per day and the owners $9. The group insurance police was increased to $25,000 and a provision was added that would allow a player's beneficiary to receive one-half of the monthly benefits for the rest of their life. Other changes were added that gave an option to receive the pension benefits at age 50 or 65, and the number of years necessary to be included in the plan was reduced to four. One of the major provisions agreed upon was the inclusion of a variable annuity policy designed to increase the amount of monthly benefits as the plan provider invested a percentage of the funds in relatively safe stocks and bonds. This proved to be a step that increased the monthly benefits over the last forty-five years or so.

Currently, the annuity fluctuates yearly and a set figure is set each July. This amount will stay locked in until the next July, when it is once again changed. Most of the time the monthly amount has increased, but there have been years when there has been a slight decrease. In 1972, a provision was added to allow retirees to take the pension as early as age 45 or as late as 65. As of 1995, players need only to be on the major league roster one day in order to receive medical and hospital benefits, and 43 days to become vested in the plan. Once a player is in the majors for 60 days, he is guaranteed a pension of $64,000 a year for life. Retired players also have the option of retaining hospital and medical parts of the plan with the cost being deducted from the monthly benefits. Players from the 1950s and 1960s draw from $25,000 to $45,000,a year depending upon years of service and the age when the pension took effect. Players from the1970s and 1980s receive in the neighborhood of $70,00 to $104,000 per year, again depending upon service and year taken. It's a great plan. The figures I listed here are estimates because actual figures are based on a year of individual service and when the player chooses to start to receive benefits.

If there's one thing the players of my generation would like to have the players of this generation do for the old timers it would be to increase the monthly pension payments for players who played from 1947 through 1965. A large number of retired players draw less than $2,000 per month and the widows draw half of that amount. Several small increases to retired players have been made but in most cases they have failed to keep up with the cost of living increases. We would like to see the increase for several reasons. First, there are a number of players from this era that through no fault of their own or because of rising medical and hospital costs have wiped out their savings and ate up their retirement checks each month. Some are in deep financial need. Two players organizations, Baseball Assistance Team (BAT) and the Major League Baseball Players Alumni Association are working hard to support these needs, but a permanent increase in their pension would go a long way in alleviating these problems. If I understand the numbers correctly this increase would barely make a dent in the pension for present day players. Players of my era may be envious of today's salaries because we cannot comprehend a minimum salary that would pay a first-year player more money than Williams and Mantle made in one year. We would however, like to see some of this money directed toward the guys who fought the early battles and won the victories that put today's players into the positive situation they have today. But these measures will need to be approved by the players and the owners.

Chapter 10
Supernovae & Twinkling Stars

O ne common denominator that runs consistent in every sport, on every team, and at every level of play, is talent. I divide talent into two categories: Supernovae are those dazzling super stars that burn so brightly in the eyes of the fans and media, and the twinkling stars shine a little less brightly, but add depth and support to the playing field. The greats in baseball are much like the real life supernovae in nearby galaxies. They are rare. But the sky is filled with a multitude of twinkling stars. So it is with baseball. Without the average star performing steadily the brilliance of the Supernovae would glow a little less bright.

I was blessed to have played with and against a multitude of greatness; Hall of Fame players, such as Ted Williams, Mickey Mantle, Yogi Berra,

Early Wynn, Ralph Kiner, Roberto Clemente, Stan Musial, Whitey Ford, Willie Mays, Nellie Fox, Willie McCovey, Ernie Banks, and Monte Irvin. The list of great stars from this era of baseball, at times, seems endless in my memory. I was honored to have been a part of baseball at this great stage of its history.

I was even more thrilled to have been a small part of an even greater number of players, major leaguers in every sense of the word, who make up the twinkling stars of the game. Volumes have been written about the Supernovae, those who have made it into the Hall of Fame. I want to focus on some of bright stars, but more on those other everyday players who had flashes of brilliance during their careers. Perhaps, circumstances changed the course of their career. Or simply, not being in the right place at the right time prevented them from taking advantage of an opportunity. Life, for each of us, holds an element of luck that elevates or relegates us to the level on which we perform and are judged.

This list of players not making it to the Hall of Fame is exceedingly longer than those who made it to Cooperstown. This journal is a tribute to those I played with or against, and friends, with whom I have maintained a personal relationship throughout the years. Those players in baseball's Hall of Fame are listed in a volume entitled, "Who's Who In Baseball." The majority of those I write of here are listed in a far more extensive volume entitled, "Who's He, In Baseball."

There seems to be at least three consistencies that are strikingly apparent in all old ballplayers. First, the inabilities to remember anything that you're suppose to do later in the day. Secondly, the amazing ability to remember every game, every inning, every pitch, hit, and throw, that took place fifty years ago. Thirdly, the presence of mind to talk baseball for endless hours, without exhaustion or having to leave the discussion for any reason, short of a coronary attack. It has been a labor of love remembering and gathering information, verifying dates, places, and facts from former teammates and journals that add depth and meaning to these stories.

Since my labors were performed sixty feet, six inches from home plate, I will begin by telling about my fellow hurlers, the workers on the mound.

Early Wynn, Pitcher

Early Wynn was one of my more famous roommates and the only one to be inducted into the Baseball Hall of Fame. Known as "Gus" by his friends and teammates, he played twenty-three seasons in the big show, and I can tell you his presence was felt in one way or another every one of those seasons.

A few years ago, Wynn was a guest on a television sports show. The host introduced him as one of the "old school," no-nonsense pitchers of his day who never hesitated to remind a hitter that he was in charge of the mound and home plate by slipping a fastball right up under his chin when the situation demanded it.

A rash of home runs were hit about this time, and Gus was asked his opinion of the curtain calls, tipping of their hats, and shaking hands with the fans that seemed to follow a home run. His response was typical of his pitching attitude: "I might knock down more of them today than I did when I pitched. In fact, I wouldn't waste a pitch on them, I'd hit them when they were still in the on-deck circle." He was big, strong, mean, ornery, tough, and in a surprising way, just as kind, gentle, and considerate.

My second start in the big leagues was in Cleveland against the Indians and Wynn. This was the only game in my baseball career that my parents and family were able to see me play in person. The game was tied 1-1 after seven. In the bottom of the eighth, the Indians had a man on first with two outs. Bobby Avila hit a high fly to deep left center. The ball was playable, but Jackie Jensen and Jimmy Piersall both hesitated at the last minute. The ball hit off Jensen's glove for an error and a run scored. Cleveland took a 2-1 lead into the ninth. Wynn set the Red Sox down in order for the victory.

The next night I was shagging balls in right field during batting practice, and Gus, who was doing wind sprints in the outfield, called me over. "Hey, kid, you threw a hell of a game last night. "He said." Sorry you had to lose it that way, but I bet you'll win plenty more before you're done. Anyway, I'm glad you took the loss and not me." Then he laughed and trotted away.

I didn't think much about it at the time, but as I reviewed facts about his career in preparation for this book, I realized that there was a possibility that had Jensen not dropped that fly ball, and Cleveland had lost that

117

Early Wynn

game, Early may not have reached that 300-win mark. Some nine years later, Gus was hanging on to a fast fading career. Following the 1962 season, Cleveland picked Wynn up from the White Sox. Gus had 299 wins, and the Indians where counting on his registering his 300th victory in a Cleveland uniform. I thought about the 2-1 game and realized that had Gus not received the win he may not have reached that magic 300 number.

Far more is written by the media highlighting the differences between owners and players than there are likenesses. There is an unwritten code in baseball that bluntly states, when a player's done, he's done. Most owners are not going to keep a player around for sentimental reasons. The attitude is, when the horse dies dismount. Potential stars are always on the horizon, someone to take a fading star's place and stir excitement with the fans. Owners do have feelings about players, some more than others, but I think it was great that the Cleveland owners gave Early the opportunity to win his 300th game in an Indians uniform, in front of the great Cleveland fans, but they did and he came through for them, himself, and baseball.

Gus could be as rough and tough as a corncob in an outhouse. He was from Indian-Scotch-Irish ancestry. On the days he was scheduled to start, he simply put on the war paint. Soon after I joined the White Sox, we took off on a two-week road trip, and I found out that I was going to room with Gus. Along with that pairing came a warning from my fellow pitching staff members, "On the day he is pitching, don't say one word to him when you get up in the morning, he'll bite your head off!" I forgot, and a few days later, sure enough, I made the mistake of asking him if he wanted to go get some breakfast. Wow! I thought all hell broke loose! I was hesitant to even look at him the rest of the day. After the game, he joined me at my locker, grabbed me by the arm and bellowed, "Come on, kid, let's get something to eat."

Another story related to Wynn came during his playing days with Cleveland. It seemed Gus was rooming alone, but the Indians signed a young pitching prospect, Sam McDowell, and rather than having the kid room alone they put him with Early. Gus' normal procedure the night before he pitched was to get himself a six-pack of beer, open the window and turn on the television, then crawl into bed. He always tried to find a western movie, preferably a John Wayne. He would drink the beer and watch the movie. When it was over, he was ready to sleep. The kid pitcher had been out experiencing big league life in the city. When he returned to the hotel, feeling pretty good, he found out he was rooming with Wynn. He was so excited he could hardly wait to get to the room. When he did, he shouted, "Mister Wynn I am so honored to be rooming with you. Let's talk baseball." He then proceeded to close the window, shut off the television, and sit on the side of Early's bed. Gus didn't say a word he picked up the phone and called the traveling secretary, "Tom, this is Early. I'm going to give you about ten minutes to change this kid's room, and if you don't I'm going to throw his stupid ass right out the window." Needless to say the room was changed quickly.

One day, I got up the courage to ask him why in heaven's name he was so angry on the day he pitched? "Ah," he said, "Yah might just say it's my war dance. I need to get fired up and convince myself those guys are taking the bread right out of my mouth. They're keeping me from buying that new car or that new house. By game time, I have a few streaks of war paint on my face and I'm ready to go to war."

I tried it a couple of times, but it didn't work for me, I'd wear myself out before the game ever started. Maybe that's why he won 300 games, and I didn't come close. Or, maybe it was because I wasn't part Indian, didn't dance very well, and was too light completed to look good in war paint.

Long after Gus hung up the spikes and glove, he was still battling in the baseball wars with the Major League Pension Committee, the owners, and the current ballplayers. He strongly believed that some of the early guys in the late Forties and Fifties had been given the short end of the stick, when it came to a decent monthly pension. He made a million phone calls, traveled to meetings at his own expense, and wrote hundreds of letters, all for one reason. He believed that the early ballplayers who contributed so much time, effort, and money to get the pension started deserved better than they were getting. You know what? He did some good, too. Some of the early players got a small increase or two. It's still not what it should be, or what it could be, but it's better than it was before Gus put on the war paint.

Wynn drove managers crazy. Pitchers have always been, and always will be, taught to stay ahead of the hitter in the count. Hitters like to get ahead of the pitchers in the count, so they can lay back and unload when he's most likely to throw his best pitch. Wynn made it to three hundred wins and the Hall of Fame by pitching behind the hitters. He also took his time. He was never in a hurry and as a result, the games he pitched always seem to last close to three hours. Gus was a highball pitcher, which not only caused managers to pace the dugout, but also kept the infielders far too relaxed. Any major league infielder will tell you that it is much easier to play behind a pitcher who is always ahead in the count than one who is constantly behind the hitters.

Gus, like the old Sinatra song, could say, "I did it my way, and I did it well." Twenty- three seasons, three hundred victories, five twenty-game winning seasons, five All-Star Games and a lifetime ERA of 3.54. He pitched in two World Series: 1954 with Cleveland and in 1959 with the Chicago White Sox. He won the Cy Young Award for Pitchers in 1959. To top this all off, he was elected to Baseball's Hall of Fame in 1972. He pitched for three teams during his career, Washington, Cleveland, and Chicago, all of the American League.

Jim Kaat, Pitcher

Jim Kaat shined brightly for twenty-five seasons over four decades and is being considered for induction in the National Baseball Hall of Fame. The Supernova joined me in Washington in 1959 as a twenty-year-old rookie, and looked even younger. As a result, he picked up the nickname, "Kitty." He never pitched one inning in the minor leagues before coming to Washington. He only pitched five innings in three games that season, so it wasn't considered his rookie year.

The big, strong, and durable pitcher was one of the best all-around athletes in baseball. He stood six feet-four inches and tipped the scales at a little over two hundred pounds. He could run, was quick and agile, like a cat. He will be remembered as one of the best fielding pitchers of all time. He won an unprecedented sixteen straight Golden Glove Awards. He could also swing the bat, banging out sixteen home runs during his career. Kaat was selected to the American League All-Star team three times, posted three, twenty-plus game winning seasons. He pitched a complete game victory over the Dodgers and Sandy Koufax in the 1965 World Series. Kitty recorded 283 victories while registering 237 losses, with a lifetime ERA of 3.45.

Kaat had back-to-back twenty-game winning seasons for the Chicago White Sox in 1974-75. He also pitched for the Phillies, the Yankees, and the 1982 World Champion St. Louis Cardinals before retiring from the

Jim Kaat

game in 1983. He was the pitching coach for the Cincinnati Reds' for two seasons before retiring and going into broadcasting. Once when Kaat was doing the color commentary for the Saturday afternoon Game of the Week, the Chicago Cubs were in the middle of a long losing streak. The game was held up due to rain, and the broadcasters were doing what they could to fill in the time during the delay. Jim's partner asked him if he had ever been on a club that experienced a long losing streak? Kitty replied, "Yes, my first season with the Senators. The team had a lengthy streak that reached about fourteen games. Russ Kemmerer pitched the fourteenth game in the streak, losing 1-0, and his single in the third inning turned out to be our only base runner. I was selected to pitch the fifteenth game mainly because no one else on the staff wanted to pitch. Russ asked manager Cookie Lavagetto if he could give me the warm up ball that is normally presented to the starting pitcher. He approached me, rubbing up the ball and said, 'Kid, I've got some good advice for you. If you want to win the game you've got to shut them out and hit a home run.' I didn't and the streak continued."

Vern Law, Pitcher

Vern Law is being considered for the Hall of Fame by the Veterans Committee. I became acquainted with Vernon through several of his Pirate teammates Dick Groat, Frank Thomas, Bob Purkey, and the Sadowski brothers, Ed and Ted. We knew each other from playing together on the Pirate All-Stars, a semi-pro traveling team, when we were growing up in Pittsburgh. These teammates and others in baseball had great respect for Vernon.

The Supernova was one of the elite National Leagues pitchers during the Fifties and Sixties. We became better acquainted during spring training and in the off- season at various sports functions in Pittsburgh. He rented my home for a couple of years during the baseball season. I had the pleasure of knowing him and I have continue to see him at various base-ball golf outings we both attend from time to time.

Law won a total of 162 games and lost 147 with the Pirates. He had an outstanding lifetime ERA of 3.77! He was also a good hitter with a re-spectable .216 batting average and 11 home runs. When you take into consideration the Pirates were one of the worst teams in baseball in the early fifties, it's easy to predict Vernon could have reached Hall of Fame

Ted Williams: 'Hey kid, just get it over the plate!'

Vern Law

numbers had he been with a winning club most of his career.

The Deacon related a story to me regarding those early Pirate teams. He said, "Life with the Pirates was most interesting. Early on, we had guys who had a hard time just playing catch without dropping the ball or making an errant throw. We invented ways to lose games, like a pop up two feet in front of home plate with the bases loaded and two out. The catcher doesn't catch the ball and because the runner knows he's out doesn't run; however, the catcher picks up the ball and instead of tagging the runner, who is standing there, throws it past first base. Our right fielder backs up the play, fields the ball, and throws it past third base. The guy who hit the ball has a grand slam home run on a ball hit two feet in front of home plate. Things like this happened much too often. As a result, we had more lineup changes than diapers on a baby. I will say that all these happenings on the field gave the team character. We learned to laugh at our mistakes and learn from them."

1960 was a great, great year for Law, the Pirates, and the city of Pittsburgh. The Pirates hadn't won a pennant since 1927. Vernon won 20 games and lost 9 with an ERA of 3.08. Two All-Star games were played that year, the purpose of which was to raise funds for the fledging major league pension plan. The first game was in Kansas City. Vernon pitched two-thirds of an inning in relief. In the second game in New York, he started for the National League, pitched two innings and was the winning pitcher in a 6-0 shutout over the American League.

The World Series between the Yankees and the Pirates was one of the most memorable series ever played. Law started the opening game, pitched seven innings, and was credited with the win. Elroy Face threw the final two innings to earn the save, as the Pirates prevailed, 6-4. The same combination worked the fourth game. Law's double and Virdon's single capped the Pirate's three-run fifth, giving them a 3 -2 lead. Vernon pitched six-and-two-third innings to gain the victory, and Face retired all eight Yankees he faced to register his second save. The series was tied three games apiece and headed for the deciding seventh game. Law started the game for the Pirates. Bob Turley started for New York, but the Pirates nicked him for two runs in the first, and they picked up two more in the second from Johnny Coates. Law limited the Yankees to one run in his five innings stint, and the Pirates led 4-1 after five innings. Bob Friend took over for the Pirates in the sixth inning, but the Yankees scored four runs to take a 5-4 lead. New York added two more in the eighth to increase the margin to 7-4. In the bottom of the eighth Pittsburgh scored five runs to take a two-run lead into the ninth, but once again the New Yorkers rallied for a pair of runs to tie the game at nine. In the bottom of the ninth, with one out, Bill homered over the left field wall, off of Ralph Terry, won the game and the World Series for Pittsburgh. Then feat is one of the greatest moments of all time in Pirate and baseball history.

1960 had to be Vernon's career highlight season, but like so many other players of this era, he's remembered as more than simply a baseball player. His nickname, "Deacon," is a tribute to his deep religious faith. A few years back Vernon's son Vance, who played in the National League for a few years with Montreal and Oakland, developed a serious blood disorder. The power of their faith, prayer and being blessed with good friends brought Vance and the Law family through the crisis. Those who played with him and those who are honored to know him understand that he is a devout person who just happened to be an outstanding baseball player.

Following his retirement from professional baseball, Vernon accepted a position as pitching coach at Brigham Young University in Provo, Utah. A few years later baseball officials from Japan began wooing him to come to Japan to coach in the professional league. They offered him a long contract. "I probably wouldn't have gone to Japan, but changes were made in the baseball program at the university, and I didn't like the direction they were heading so I accepted the offer to go to Japan" Vernon explained. The Japanese officials wanted him to commit to a ten-year contract, but he convinced them that a yearly contract would be best for both parties since there was no guarantee that he would be happy living in Japan, or they would like his coaching style. He insisted a clause agreeing that they pay both in Japanese and American taxes in addition to his coaching salary. When the interpreter assured Vern that the contract had all the t's crossed and the i's dotted, he signed.

As the season progressed, Law continued to ask the interpreter if both taxes were being paid. His answer was always the same. "Oh, yes, Lawson, everything is taken care of." As the season neared its end, Vernon asked him again about the taxes and reminded him that he would have to take written proof to the U.S. Embassy showing his taxes had been paid. "Okay, Law-son, I'll get them!" the interpreter assured. The next day he was informed that only the Japanese taxes had been paid and he would be required to pay the U.S. taxes.

"As it turned out, it cost me practically all of the $50,000 I made so, in reality, I worked the whole season for nothing," he commented. I did learn one thing from the experience, if you are going to work with these people you better have a sharp pencil and a good lawyer.

"There are a lot of excellent players in Japan, and I enjoyed working with the young players. One needs only to look at the number of Japanese players that have been signed by our professional teams and are doing well in the major leagues to understand that they are talented.

"It's a totally different world over there! The Japanese philosophy of baseball is the exact opposite of our approach in this country. The system is militaristic and the maneuvers of punishment for poor performances verge on humiliation. There is no room for individuality. Everyone has to do things together, all in step and in cadence. Pitchers have to develop the same motion and hitters the same swing. Anyone out of step, like a nail, is hammered down. Catchers are often taken behind the dugout and beat around severely enough to draw blood for calling the wrong pitches. Pitchers, who fail to survive the first inning have been required to kneel on the cement dugout floor and not move for the rest of the game, or sent to the batting cage to throw into the net for two hours, or required to field a shopping cart full of baseball hit by one of the coaches from left field to right until the cart is empty or the player dropped from exhaustion.

"Pitchers are required to throw everyday. A pitcher may throw 35 minutes of batting practice, be scheduled for duty in the bullpen, and warm up two or three times during the early part of the game. Then he may be called into the game in the seventh inning and pitch the last three innings. He's rewarded by starting the game the following night and pitching six good innings. Then the following night he's back in the bullpen again. The thinking of the management and coaches is that if pitchers aren't working everyday they are cheating their employer. They don't seem to understand that throwing a baseball is unnatural and in order for a pitcher to be effective his arm and body must have rest.

"To the Japanese, practice is more important than the game. Practice is held three to four hours prior to the game. They are competitive, designed to decide who will play and who will sit. If you don't practice hard you don't play in the game. With this kind of schedule, it is impossible to be up and competitive for every game, because by the time the game starts players are so tired they just want to sit and rest. If there was anything good I accomplished as a coach in Japan, it was my insistence that the pre-game practices be changed to a warm-up approach rather than competition to see who plays, and that pitchers be given time to rest their arms between outings."

"I never did adjust to the embarrassment inflicted upon the player who made an error, and was immediately removed from the game. I remember a third baseman for the Seibu Lions who had great potential but never reached it because he knew before the game that he would be embarrassed by the manager at every opportunity. He got to the point he hated he game.

"One other thing I remember about Japanese baseball, it was very predictable! Pitchers would always throw the same pitch with the same count, one ball one strike, or two and two, three and one. Managers always called the take sign in similar situations, and they always called for a bunt in the same circumstances. I can't remember a 1-0 game mainly because the pitchers threw so much they were tired and everyone knew what the next pitch or strategy was going to be.

"Baseball in Japan was more than just a world away for the American players who choose to show their talents in the Far East. Life in Japan can be lonely, the adjustment to the culture difficult, the focus on the game itself misunderstood, and the language barrier impossible. Life can be lonely!"

Camilo Pascual, Pitcher

The Veterans Committee is also considering Camilo Pascual for the Hall of Fame. Whenever baseball hitters talk about a curveball, the name of Pascual leaps into the conversation. The soft-spoken Supernova was a teammate of mine with the Senators for four seasons.

Without a doubt the Cuban had the most feared curveball in the American League for 18 years. Camilo had a direct overhand delivery and a high leg kick that shielded the ball from the hitter until the last possible moment. To make it even more deceptive, he twisted his body around almost to second base before delivering the ball to the plate. Pascual had a blazing fastball that he kept high in the strike zone. His curve started out at the same level as his fastball and broke straight down ending up about knee high. He was almost impossible to hit. He led the American League

Camilo Pascual

in strikeouts three years in a row, 1961-63, which is a testimony as to how good he really was. He also led the league in shutouts and complete games on three different occasions. He was 17-10 with an ERA of 2.64 in 1959. That year the Senators only won 63 games.

Pascual ended his career with 174 wins and 106 losses, a winning percentage of .621 on a team that was in the American League cellar most of his career. His lifetime earned run average was a more than respectable 3.63 and his 2,167 strikeouts put him in a special class. When I began writing this section of the book, my goal was to concentrate on players who had long successful careers, but for one reason or another would not be voted into the Hall of Fame. If there ever was a player, in this case a pitcher, it's Camilo Pascual!

The Senators knew they had a jewel. Every club in the league wanted this talented Cuban, but Clark Griffith held onto his prize pitcher. In twelve of his 18 seasons he posted winning numbers. I wonder what Camilo's numbers would be if he had been with the Yankees during the same time period he was with Washington. He was in the wrong place at the wrong time. Pascual was as good a right-handed pitcher as there was in the American League in the Fifties and Sixties.

Sports announcers and those who decided on those who are chosen to be in the Hall of Fame probably never saw Pascual pitch will brush his numbers off as not getting 300 wins. But if we could get the opinions of the great hitters in the American League during the time that Camilo pitched, I would bet the farm that man to man they would be in agreement that he was as good a pitcher as there was in baseball.

Billy Pierce, Pitcher

Billy Pierce is also being considered for induction by the Veterans Committee. The left-handed pitcher and was a former teammate of mine with the Chicago White Sox. Billy's career covered 18 years with the three different teams: Detroit Tigers, Chicago, and San Francisco Giants. His credentials list 211 victories and 169 losses, with a sparkling career ERA of 3.27.

He is the only starting pitcher selected to seven All-Star teams, who is not in the Hall of Fame. Like Carl Hubbell, Grover Alexander, Bob Gibson, and Greg Maddux, Pierce led his decade (1950s) in ERA. His victory total of 211 games surpasses the total games won by Chief Bender,

Billy Pierce

Dizzy Dean, Don Drysdale, Jess Haines, Sandy Koufax, Bob Lemon, Hal Newhouser, Rube Marquard, and Sandy Vance, and places him among the top 80 pitchers in the history of the major leagues. Billy threw thirty-eight shutouts, and struck out 1,199 hitters, which places him in the top fifty pitchers in history. He quietly, without a great deal of notice from the media, became the best left-handed pitcher with the most wins in the American League during the Fifties. Three times during the decade, he led the league in complete games. He went to the San Francisco Gaints in 1962 and helped the team to the World Series with his 16-6 record. Then he was 1-1 in the Series.

Pierce came close to pitching two no-hitters in 1958. Both games were against the Washington Senators. The scores were identical. In the first game, playing in Chicago in late June, Billy pitched eight and two-thirds innings of perfect ball against the Senators and had two strikes on Eddie Fitzgerald, who came into the game as a pinch-hitter in the ninth inning. Fitzgerald hit a soft Texas leaguer, just inside the right field foul line to ruin the perfect game. A few weeks later in Washington, Billy pitched another one hitter, 3-0 victory over the Senators.

Pierce, along with Nellie Fox and Sherman Lollar, were the leaders of the "Go-Go Sox." They led by example, temperament, and inspiration! I joined the White Sox early in the 1960 season. During a road trip, several of us were sitting in the hotel lobby talking baseball, and that almost perfect game came up. I mentioned that most of the Senators were sorry that Pierce didn't get that perfect game. We were well out of the pennant race by that time and it was just another game chalked up in the loss column.

I said, "I bet he was really upset not getting the perfect game?"

"No," someone said. "He reacted as he always did following a win. He gave credit to the team for their great defense and scratching out the winning run, and credit to the Senators for a tough game. He showed no great emotion or bitterness. He took a shower, dressed, and went home to his family."

"Well," I said, "it would have bothered me. I would have been happy with the way I pitched, and the win, but I bet I would have moaned for a month about losing the perfect game."

That was the type of leading by example that kept the Sox cool and capable for the next few seasons. Oh, by the way, I did have an interest in both of Bill's one hitters that year. I pitched against the Sox and was shut out by Pierce, and was the loser in both of those game.

Virgil Trucks, Pitcher

Yet another pitcher being considered by the Veterans Committee is Virgil Trucks. Although I never played with or against Virgil, I knew who he was along with his reputation as a tough pitcher with a great record. Several years ago we were introduced to each other at a golf outing in Indiana. Our friendship blossomed quickly and has grown during the passing years. It has continued to grow and holds great value to us both! We speak on the telephone every couple of weeks, and we are blessed to be able to visit each other and take part in several golf outings each year.

One such outing we both greatly enjoy taking part in is the Catoosa County Special Olympics, which has been held for the past 27 years in Ringgold, Georgia. The outing's purpose was to raise much-needed funds and awareness of students with Downs-syndrome deficiency. The two-day event included visiting the "Special Olympians" at their schools. Virgil and I were partners visiting one of the high schools. The young people put on their rendition of *Sleeping Beauty*. It turned out to be one of those unexpected, rewarding moments that flood your brain with memories. Perhaps it was because my years of teaching made me realize how extremely difficult it was for these particular students and their teachers. You could sense the nervousness of these youngsters as they listened to last-minute instructions from their teachers. The whole student body plus special guest would be watching. They had to memorize their lines, remember their clues, and act out their parts. This is a tall order for any young student. For these children it was a mountain to climb. They pulled it off without a hitch well almost. The witch tripped over her broomstick, which brought a snicker from the cast and audience, and encouragement from the teacher. They did a great job! When it was over you could see the pressure leave, the smiles return to their faces, and a sense of pride flood their being. I felt a degree of happiness that could not have been more sincere had they been my own children. Virgil and I are both looking forward to many return visits.

Virgil was consistently among the league leaders, and he is one of five pitchers in baseball history to throw two no-hitters in one season. The

Virgil Trucks

others are Johnny Vander Meer, Allie Reynolds, Jim Maloney, and Nolan Ryan. Virgil is the only one of the five to pitch both no-hitters in the afternoon. One might ask, what difference does it makes whether the no hitters were pitched at night or during the day? Any major league hitter will attest to the difference in hitting in a day or night game. At night, with the lights focused down on the playing field, hitters see the upper half of the baseball once the pitcher releases it. In the daytime, you get a better view of the whole baseball because the sunlight brightens the top of the ball and the light is reflected up from the field making the whole baseball easier to see. Ted Williams once remarked that he believed the single most difficult thing to do in all of sports was to squarely hit a round ball on a round bat, coming toward you at 90 to 100 miles an hour. Take my word for it, daytime baseball makes hitting a bit easier.

Pitching for Detroit in 1952, Trucks shut out the Washington Senators 1-0 on May 15, and on August 25th, he shut out the Yankees 1-0. This second no-hitter was mildly contested by the official scorer and the other media in the press box. In the third inning, the Yankee's shortstop, Phil Rizzuto, hit a ball up the middle. Johnny Pesky, the Tiger's second baseman, fielded the ball but was unable to get a grip on it as it rolled around in his glove. Rizzuto was called safe on a close play at first that was heatedly questioned by the Detroit players. It was scored a hit by the official scorer, but contested by the other members of the press. At the end of the fourth inning, a call was made to the Tiger's bench, and Pesky was asked his opinion. Pesky replied without hesitation, "The ball was rolling around in my glove it was an error all the way!" The mistake was corrected both on the official score sheet and on the scoreboard, and as a result Virgil had his second no-hitter of the season.

In February 2002, I was attending an induction ceremony at the Ted Williams Museum and both Trucks and Pesky were in attendance. Trucks was being inducted into Ted's Wall of Great Achievement. One evening we were sitting around doing what old ballplayers love to do, talk about baseball, and I brought up the subject of Virgil's second no-hitter. Without blinking an eye, Johnny said, "It was an error all the way, no doubt about it. The ball rolled around in my glove, it would have been an easy out had I fielded it cleanly."

One other tidbit from the 1952 season is that Virgil nearly had a third no-hitter. Late in the season pitching against the Senators, Eddie Yost, the lead off hitter for Washington, singled to left field. As it turned out he was the only Senator to reach base that day.

Virgil had several fantastic accomplishments in the minor leagues. He pitched two no-hitters for Andalusia of the Alabama-Florida League in 1938, and two more for Beaumont of the Texas League in 1940, and another for Buffalo of the International League in 1941. Trucks obtained the nickname of "Fire," while pitching for Andalusia.

Trucks was named to the American League All-Star team in 1949 and again in 1954. He was credited with one win and one save. Virgil has a unique distinction. He is the answer to one of baseball's great trivia questions: Name one pitcher who won more games in the World Series than he did during the regular season. In 1945, just back from military service, Trucks pitched a complete game beating, the Cubs 4-1 in the second game of the series.

During his career, he twice led the league in shutouts and once led the league in strikeouts. His final record was 177-135 with a 3.39 ERA. His records seem even more impressive when you consider he established the stats on teams that averaged a .505 winning percentage. He also gave two years out of his career to serve his country in the Second World War. I don't know if the quality of a player's character is even a consideration in determining his value to baseball's history, but if it is, then without a doubt, he should be in Baseball's Hall of Fame. I don't know of anyone who represents the game of baseball with more integrity and respect than Virgil Trucks.

Elden Auker, Pitcher

My first choice for "Twinkling Stars" is one of those special people who through the grace of God happens into a life, and instantly developed into a relationship so pure, powerful, and blessed that had you never experienced it would leave a void in your life. Such a person is Elden Auker.

Elden was playing in the major leagues with Detroit in 1933 when I was just two years old. He pitched ten seasons in the majors with Detroit, Boston, and St. Louis in the American League. Elden won 130 games during his career and lost 101. His lifetime ERA was 4.42.

In Game Four of the 1934 World Series, he pitched a complete game and was the winning pitcher in a 10-4 victory over the St. Louis Cardinals.

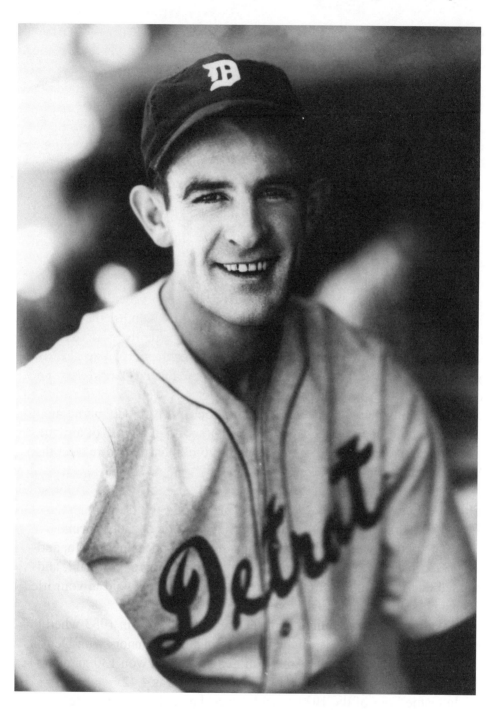

Elden Auker

He was the losing pitcher in game seven as Dizzy Dean shut out the Tigers 11-0. He pitched six innings against the Chicago Cubs in the third game of the 1935 World Series, but was not the pitcher of record.

I met Elden several years ago at the Ted Williams Museum. Elden and Williams became teammates in 1939. In February of 1998, Elden and I were both invited to attend the Museum ceremonies and were introduced for the first time. One evening, someone raised the subject of ex-major league baseball players being used to celebrity treatment. Elden chuckled, then told a story about his return to his hometown Norcatur, Kansas, following the 1934 World Series. He and his wife Mildred decided it would be best to return home quietly, at night, to prevent any fanfare that might occur if their arrival were announced in advance. They envisioned school being dismissed, a parade, the band, and the whole town turning out to applaud the hometown athletic hero who had just won the fourth game of the World Series. So return at night they did. Elden's father was a postman and Elden decided to walk the route with his father the morning following their arrival. As they entered the post office, the Postmaster who welcomed Elden with open arms and these words greeted them, "Elden, we sure missed you this summer! Where in the name of heaven have you been?"

Elden laughed and said, "Talk about celebrity treatment and having the wind knocked out of your sails. I'll tell you, I was brought back to reality in a hurry. The town, for the most part, didn't even realize I pitched in a World Series, or that it had even been played."

Elden was a three-sport All-American at Kansas State University, and was voted All Big Six. He was working on a medical degree when the call of "play ball" changed the direction of his life.

This was the beginning of our friendship. Later that year, we met in Indianapolis where he was to receive an award from industry for his many contributions and services. On June 11, 1999, we were both invited to attend a ceremony at Shea Stadium. It was the 60th anniversary of Ted Williams debut into the major leagues. Elden and I, along with Ted's other guest, spoke of our gratitude at being included in this fantastic event honoring the greatest hitter that ever played the game.

Elden was 90 years old on September 21, 2000. On November 4th a group of former players, close friends, and family joined Elden and Mildred to celebrate this occasion. Tommy Lasorda was to be the Master of Ceremonies, but his duties as vice president of the Los Angeles Dodgers made it impossible for him to attend. I was more than honored when asked to pinch-hit for him. It turned out to be a very enjoyable evening! I was accustomed to public speaking, but truthfully, standing there in front of so many peers from professional sports, government, and big business, had me a little on edge. John McHale, former owner of the Detroit Tigers, Mrs. Joe Cronin, and her daughter Maureen, were a few names in attendance. The Cronin's were close friends of the Aukers. Cronin was the general manager of the Red Sox when I first joined the organization. Maureen was a teenager, who along with her three brothers, was often in attendance at Fenway during the season. I had met Mrs. Cronin one time during my stay in Boston. I had dinner at the front table with the Cronin's, and our conversation drifted to Calvin Griffith, Marlene's uncle, who was the owner of the Washington Senators during my years there. She asked me to be sure to mention him in a positive way in this journal.

When the last game was played at Briggs Stadium in Detroit, it was Auker who spoke for all the former Tiger players. His closing remarks regarding the fabled history of the stadium, great accomplishments of players and outstanding teams, memories seeped in baseball tradition, and loyal fans whose love and support made Tiger baseball the class of the American League, brought tears to the eyes of all who attended.

We have a tendency to place people in categories especially, athletes or celebrities from all walks of life, because of the roles they play or their contributions made to the profession they embraced. They are remembered by the impressions left, as a mark of identification. Far too often, the true value of a person is hidden by these marks. Elden Auker was a better-than-average-baseball player. He is a far better human being than he ever was a player, and if you asked him, how he would like to be remembered, I'm positive his reply would be, as a good husband and father, a God-fearing man, a good friend, a considerate human being, and a person who contributed to the betterment of the human race. One thing is certain in my mind, when Elden crosses over the river of life, and his Lord will be there to meet him on the other side and mark "well done" beside his name in the scorebook of life.

Frank Baumann, Pitcher

Frank Baumann was one of the gifted "Big Bonus Babies" of the early 1950's. He was from St. Louis, and Boston signed him right out of high school in 1952 for a bonus reported to be at $100,000. Frank joined the Louisville Colonels of the American Association for the remainder of the season. He was impressive with a fastball in the mid-ninety's, and a fair curve ball. He appeared in 15 games, pitched 88 innings, registered four wins and six losses, struck out 69 batters and had an ERA of 4.09. Not bad numbers for a kid making the jump from high school to Triple-A baseball. Baumann was another of a long list of players signed by the Red Sox, that Boston gave up on too early. He continued his career successfully with other teams.

Soon after signing with Boston, Frank married his childhood sweetheart who was 16 years old. Frank was a rusty old 18 at the time. Not only was he young, but also one of the most gullible people I had ever met. The Louisville club at that time was made up of a combination of older experienced veterans and young prospects. It didn't take long for the old pros to take advantage of Frank's willingness to believe the sky was falling. They would send him after the groundskeeper to see if he had a left-handed monkey wrench, or explain to him why it was necessary when we traveled to keep his left arm in the net that hung in the sleeping cars.

Without doubt the worst-prank played on Frank was the information they gave him related to his pitching assignments and his sexual habits. A great rumor floated around in those days about athletes that indulged in sex prior to a game would lose their stamina. Frank was in the starting five-day pitching rotation, which meant starting a game on Monday resting on Tuesday, throwing a little batting practice or working with a catcher on the side Wednesday, resting on Thursday and starting the game on Friday. The boys convinced Frank that he should not have sex two days prior to starting a game and two after he pitched in a game. The information was relayed to Frank the week before we were scheduled for a two-week road trip, and two days before Frank had a scheduled start. Keep in mind now that Frank and his young wife had just been married. Well, it doesn't take a math professor to figure out that Frank and his young wife were not physically enjoying much of each others company on a regular basis, and you could see the tension mounting in Frank's nature as time passed. He became short tempered, strong headed, frustrated and you name the rest.

Frank Baumann

One day we were rained out at home and while waiting for the downpour to stop Frank cornered Al Curtis, Bob Smith, and me to find out how we handled this abstinence routine. By the time he had finished explaining his dilemma, we were all rolling on the floor laughing with tears flowing down our cheeks. As gullible as Frank was, it didn't take him to long to decide he had been taken for a joy ride. He looked and acted a lot better the next day, and I am sure his wife was also relieved. Experience is still the best tool of education.

The following year Baumann posted great numbers at Louisville. He won 10, lost 1, had an earned run average of 2.55, and struck out 95 hitters in 106 innings. He was on his way to Boston, but instead was drafted and spent 1954 in the military. After that he was with Boston in 1955 and 1956. He pitched in only seven games both of those seasons. He floated between Boston and the minors for the next couple of seasons posting minimal numbers and was finally traded to the White Sox in 1960. White Sox pitching coach Ray Berres changed Frank's delivery from a sidearm to a three-quarter. It worked wonders! Baumann posted a 13-6 record, with an ERA of 2.85 in 47 games and 185 innings pitched. Frank remained with the Chicago through 1964 but never registered big numbers. He then moved across town to the Cubs in 1965 and finished his career there. He now resides in St. Louis with his family.

Joe Black, Pitcher

My attention was drawn to an article in the sports section of the Indianapolis Star on Saturday, May 18, 2002, listing the death of Joe Black. I had not planned on mentioning Joe simply because he and I were teammates with Washington for only a short part of the 1957 season.

Joe came up with the Brooklyn Dodgers in 1952. He was used mostly in relief because of his overpowering fastball and a tireless arm that permitted him to pitch well several days in a row when needed. He won fifteen games for the National League Champions that year and saved another fifteen out of the bullpen and only had four losses. His 2.15 ERA and .789 winning percentage were enough for him to be named the National League Rookie of the Year. Joe was the first black pitcher in baseball history to win a World Series game. He beat the Yankees and Allie Reynolds, 4-2, in the first game of the series.

Joe Black

Ike Delock

Black was with the Dodgers until 1955 then was traded to the Cincinnati Reds. In 1957, the Senators signed Joe in hopes that he would be able to help the bullpen and save a few games for the starting pitchers: Camilo Pascual, Pedro Ramos, Chuck Stobbs, Truman Clevenger, and me.

Cal Griffith wanted to see what Joe had left so he started him a few days after his arrival in Washington. Black had never been in the American League and was not familiar with the hitters. We didn't have a lot of pre-game meetings in those days to go over the opposing hitters, so Joe asked me to help him with how to pitch to each batter, and we worked out a system. As each hitter came to the plate, I would signal Joe the best location to pitch the hitters. If he were a highball hitter, I would touch some part of my body below my belt, signaling him to keep the ball down. If the hitter were a low-ball hitter, I would touch above my belt. If I wanted the ball inside I would rub my chest. If I wanted it away, I would reach out my hand. Joe pitched seven good innings and although we lost a close 2-1 game Joe felt he had done well enough to at least get another opportunity to pitch. He came over to my locker after the game to express his gratitude and said, "Russ, the first time we get to New York, I am going to take you to Harlem, and after that experience you will never want to be white again!" I laughed because Joe had heard that I like jazz and blues music and that's why he made the suggestion. To be truthful, I looked forward to the experience but we never had the opportunity to carry through with it. Joe pitched five more innings for the Senators and was released before we ever got to New York.

Ike Delock Pitcher

Ike Delock, another Boston teammate, is the next member to be introduced as a "Twinkling Star." Ivan, which was his real first name, had a pitching career that lasted a eleven seasons, all of it in a Boston uniform, except for a brief stint with Baltimore at the end of his career. He won 84 games and lost 75. His career ERA was a respectable 4.04. And in 1956, he led the American League in wins for a relief pitcher.

Ike was a tough customer, a former Marine with a no-give-or-take attitude. The fact that he served in the Marines made him a favorite of Ted Williams since he served two hitches as a Marine pilot. Delock battled every hitter and never gave an inch. Ted Williams often asked Ike how he would pitch him. Ike's reply was always the same, "Hey, I'm not telling you anything, if there is a trade I'm the one that will be traded, and you want me to tell you how I'd pitch you? No way!"

Williams asked the question once too often and Ike finally replied. "Okay, Okay," I'll tell you how I'd pitch you. The first pitch would be right under your chin, and the second, I'd drill you right on the knee cap!" Ted merely shook his head and walked away.

I've always felt that had Ike pitched against Ted, he would have pitched him just the way he said he would. Not only was Ike tough, but also he was one of the best-dressed players in the majors, a sharp guy! I have the good fortune of retaining my friendship with Ike through the years, and we normally see each other at golf outings several times a year. Good friends are hard to come by.

Ned Garver, Pitcher

Another Twinkling Star pitcher was Ned Garver, a pitcher on the 1951 American League All-Star Team who played 14 years in the majors with the Browns, Tigers, Royals and Angels. His career win-and-loss record was 129-157, with a respectable ERA of 3.73.

In 1952, the St. Louis only won 52 games. Ned was credited with 20 of those victories and he registered just 11 of the teams 102 losses. Had there been a Cy Young Award for pitchers established at this time, Garver would have been a hands-down favorite to win the award. Not only did he lead the team in pitching victories, he also batted a team leading .305. As it turned out, he was runner up to Yogi Berra of the Yankees in the MVP voting. Ned had the reputation of being a tough pitcher to beat. He seldom gave into the hitter and he protected the inside part of the plate with the good old- fashion chin music.

Ned and I have continued our friendship over the years. We play in several of the same golf outings, and not long ago we were guest on a unique panel show in Indianapolis, along with Carl Erskine and Bernie Allen. Prior to the dinner, the audience was asked to prepare questions for the panel members. Unless the question was specifically directed to one member, each of us had an opportunity to respond. The program had a one-hour limit, but it lasted nearly three hours because each of us seemed to have a response to most of the questions. One particular question concerned the attitude of the modern hitters regarded being brushed back by pitchers. Today, pitches toward the inside part of the plate produce

Ned Garver

Dick Hyde

glares and stares and umpire's warnings. In our time, pitchers were expected to pitch inside and protect their players. Garver responded, "If I were pitching today the games would take four hours, two hours for the game and another two hours to stop the fighting!"

Dick Hyde, Pitcher

Dick Hyde is perhaps the best example I can give of a player having flashes of brilliance in a career circumvented by circumstances, or just plain bad luck. "Snake," as he was nicknamed because his underhanded-side-arm delivery, seemed to worm his way from the mound to home plate. He was the top relief pitcher in the American League in 1958. That season he posted a 10-3 record with 19 saves and a earned run average of 1.75 for a team that finished as always, first in war, first in peace, and last in the American League.

Hyde spent seven years toiling in the minor leagues, then spent two more years in the military before making it to the Senators in 1957. Then came the brilliant 1958 season. Every team in baseball wanted to trade for his services, even the Yankees. Cal Griffith made the decision to hold onto this valuable piece of baseball property. Dick developed arm trouble the following spring and his sensational season was never to be repeated. Griffith tried to trade him to the Boston Red Sox the following spring training, but Snake was unable to pass the physical exam and was returned to the Senators. Washington released him in 1960.

Underhand pitchers seldom, if ever have arm trouble. Usually, there is little or no strain on the shoulder or elbow. This is one reason fast-pitch softball pitchers, both male and female, can pitch everyday. What is it about fate that lifts a person from the path of mediocrity, feeds them a spoonful of brilliance, only to snatch it back just as they begin to savor the taste? Hyde is just one of a nameless number who has experienced the trap. He ended his six-year career with a record of 17 wins, 14 defeats, and a 3.56 earned run average.

Snake and I were road roommates for a couple of seasons. He was a delightful person, always happy, a grin on his face all the time. I don't ever remember seeing him angry, upset, or bitter toward anyone. He had a live, vivid sense of humor, almost to the point of being ridiculous at times. We were in New York for a weekend series with the Yankees. Night games in those days started around eight o'clock. It was customary following batting and infield practice on a Friday night, for the visiting team to send the starting pitcher for Saturday's day game back to the hotel so he could get a decent meal and hop into bed early enough for a reasonable nights rest. More often than not, even with a quick game, it was long after midnight before teams would get back to the hotel.

Since I was scheduled to start the Saturday game, I followed this routine and returned to the hotel. I was watching the game on television, but along about the fifth inning there was a knock at the door. I opened it to find a beautiful women standing there smiling. She asked if I was Russ Kemmerer, and explained that she had been in Louisville, Kentucky, for the Derby, and met a former minor league teammate of mine who suggested if she was ever in New York when the Senators were in town to look me up. Since she was in the Big Apple on a modeling assignment, and the Senators were indeed in town, she decided to follow that very suggestion made by my friend and look me up. I invited her into the room and she continued with her explanation. She had gone to Yankee Stadium and just happened to lean over the bullpen fence and ask one of the Senators, who just happened to be Hyde, if he would introduce me to her. Snake told her I was back at the hotel, gave her the room number.

We chatted for awhile and she asked if we could go and get something to eat. The game was over by that time and I suddenly understood how extremely difficult it was for a grown man to try to explain to a beautiful grown women, why he couldn't leave the hotel because he was pitching in a baseball game tomorrow, and had been sent back to his hotel to get his rest, and that leaving the hotel for any reason would be breaking curfew, and result in a fine. She didn't really understand my explanation but suggested room service. That failed also because they had closed. She finally asked if I would walk her to the elevator. I agreed that I would leave her a ticket for tomorrow's game. As the elevator doors opened she said good night and watched as I turned a sickly green color. I did so because

Our manager, Cookie Lavagetto and our pitching coach, Walter Beck, departed from the elevator as the young lady was about to entered. As the elevator doors closed, I blurted out, "Cookie, it's not what you think."

"Well," he replied. "I hope you had a great evening because it going to cost you $200 bucks!"

I responded, "It was a joke. Hyde sent her up to the room!"

150

"Hey! I got a pretty good look at her and she didn't look like a joke to me."

I knew it was hopeless to try to convince him of my innocence. Later in the room, I told Dick what happened and pleaded with him to explain the situation to Lavagetto. He just smiled and said, "Hey roomy, I never laid eyes on her."

The next afternoon I was having trouble with the Yankees. Along about the fifth inning, Cookie came out to the mound to take me out of the game. "You look tired" to me," he quipped. "I better get you out of here so you can go back to the hotel and get a little rest; evidently you didn't get much rest last night!"

"Come on skip, I didn't do a damn thing but talk to that women!"

He responded, "Your not that dumb, How stupid do you think I am? The $200 buck will come out of your next check."

I never did see that women again, and Hyde, in his subtle humorous manner, never did tell Cookie the full story. He thought it was funny and did not believe they would fine me.

A few years later I had been traded to Houston. We were in New York playing the Mets in a day-night double-header. Lavagetto was then a coach under Casey Stengel with the Mets. I was mostly relieving by this time in my career. I came into the afternoon contest along about the seventh inning with the score tied. We ended up beating the Mets in the top of the ninth. That evening I entered the game in the seventh inning again, and gained my second victory of the day as we defeated the Mets for the second time that day.

The Mets, at that time were playing in the old Polo Grounds. The locker rooms for both teams were located in centerfield. As I header for the locker room I hear a voice calling, "Hey Dutch, wait up." It was Cookie. He congratulated me on my double victory and expressed how well he thought I was throwing the ball.

Finally, I stopped, looked him in the eye and said, "Skipper, do you remember fining me for being with that women a couple of years ago?"

"Stop, if you're going to tell me that you were innocent then I only have one thing to say. I didn't believe you then, and I don't believe you now!

Ellis Kinder, Pitcher

Ellis Kinder, a Boston teammate, is more than just a "Twinkling Star" because he was the first of a kind true relief pitcher converted from a starter. Ellis was tagged with the nickname, "Old Folks," because he didn't start his baseball career until he was 24 years old in 1938. He made it to the majors in 1946 with the St. Louis Browns at the age of 34. After a tour of duty in WW II with the Navy, he came to the Red Sox in a trade prior to the 1948 season. In 1949, "Ellie" won 23 games and lost six for a league leading winning percentage of .793. He also led the league with six shutouts. Oddly enough, he was not selected to the American League All-Star Team that year. The 23 wins were the most he had in any single season. The next season he was converted to more of a reliever.

His arm kept him out of the starting rotation more than anything else. Most pitchers take ten to fifteen minutes to warm up the arm prior to pitching. Ellis, for some reason, could be ready to go into a game after throwing three or four pitches.

During my rookie season, Ellis spent almost all of his time in the Boston bullpen. He would find a place in the corner of the bench and doze off. If the game was close from the seventh inning on, our pitching coach, Paul Schreiber, would nudge Ellis awake, and sure enough, if he was needed, he would throw three or four pitches and walk to the mound. As a result of this ability, it soon became apparent that his value to the Red Sox would be in the number of times he could come into a game rather than

Mel Parnell, Pitcher

Mel Parnell was another pitcher and former Red Sox teammate. The Twinkling Star was also an American League All Star in 1949 and 1951. Mel pitched for ten years with the Red Sox, and is listed as one of the all-time great lefthanders in Boston history. He won 123 games and lost 75 in his career and posted a 3.50 ERA. His best season came in 1949, when Mel won 25 games and lost seven with an ERA of 2.77. He again posted a 20-win season in 1953, winning 21, while losing seven and posting an ERA of 3.06.

With two 20-game winning seasons under his belt, Mel was looking for a great year in 1954. However, on April 24, he was hit by a pitch from Washington pitcher, Maurice McDermott, that broke his arm and for all

Ellis Kinder

Mel Parnell

practical purpose ended Mel's career. Parnell won three games after his return to the active list near the end of the season, and in his final two seasons with the Boston was limited to nine victories.

Mel and I were reunited a few years back at a golf outing. He greeted me with a warm handshake and recalled the time I hit Karl Drews of the Phillies in retaliation for hitting Sammy White of Boston. "You gained a great deal of respect that day simply because you gave both teams the message that even though you were a rookie, you were willing to protect your teammates," he said.

In 1951, he set the major league record by appearing in sixty-three games. And he led American League relievers in wins, 10, and saves, 14. He set a new record in 1953 when he appeared in sixty-nine games. He again led league relievers with wins, 10, and saves, 27. His ERA that season was a career low of 1.85! During his career, he won 107 games, lost 71, saved 102, and had an ERA of 3.43.

He then spoke of another game. "Later that year, you came in to relieve me in the sixth inning at Yankee Stadium. The tying runs were on base with one out and Mickey Mantle and Yogi Berra coming to the plate. You got Mantle out on strikes and Berra on a fly ball to center. You shut the Yankees down the next three innings and saved the game."

Mel invited several friends and me to celebrate the event at a nightclub in New Jersey. The Tommy and Jimmy Dorsey Band were in concert. After the show I was introduced to both brothers and their manager, and I was privileged to get to know them and visit with them several times during my career.

Herb Score, Pitcher

Many baseball people believed Herb Score had the ability to go down in baseball history as one of the most talented left-handed pitchers of all time. I only saw one other lefty during my days in the American League I thought had equal or better stuff than Herb and that was Mickey McDermott of the Red Sox. Strangely enough, both of these talented pitchers, for one reason or another, never reached their potential.

I first became aware of Score in 1954 when he was pitching for the Indianapolis Indians and I was hurling for Louisville in the American Association.

Early in May, Score was leading the league in wins, and I was leading

Herb Score

the league in earned run average. Score and I went head to head against each other the day I made my final appearance that year for Louisville. I won the contest 6-2 and the Red Sox called me up to the parent club. Herb went on to register a 22-5 season with an ERA of 2.62. He pitched 251 innings, gave up only 140 hits and struck out 330 hitters. He was promoted the following year to the Cleveland Indians where he put together a 16-10 record with 245 strikeouts and a 2.85 ERA the American League Champions. He bettered those numbers in 1956 winning 20 and losing 9 with a 2.53 ERA and 263 strikeouts.

In May of 1957, Score was pitching against the Yankees. Second baseman Gil McDougald lined a shot that struck Herb squarely in the right eye. The injury proved to be severe, and Score's immediate battle was saving his eye. Herb didn't pitch the rest of the season and for all practical purposes his career was over. He did recover from the injury, but for some reason never recovered his confidence. He won just 17 games over the final five years of his career.

I was a teammate of Score's for three years with the White Sox. Al Lopez, who had been Herb's manager in Cleveland, nurtured him along slowly and gave him the opportunity to regain the confidence he had in Cleveland, but it just never happened. Herb, when you watched him throw, seemed to have the same speed and good breaking ball he possessed prior to the injury, but he just never regained his winning ways.

I believe Score would have gone down in baseball as one of the best left-handed pitchers of all time had the injury not occurred. His injury along with the broken toe Dizzy Dean suffered in the All-Star game that shortened his career must go down in baseball as one of the most tragic injuries of all time. He ended up winning 55 games and losing 46. In all seriousness his numbers could easily have been 300 and 146, and a place in Cooperstown.

Chuck Stobbs, Pitcher

The Boston Red Sox signed Chuck Stobbs right out of high school. He made his major league debut at the age of 18. He had three straight winning seasons with Boston then was traded to the Chicago White Sox then the Washington Senators.

Chuck made his first start for the Senator's in front of the hometown crowd and instantly became a topic of conversation because he gave up

Mickey Mantle's legendary 565-foot home run. On my first trip to Washington, during my rookie season in 1954, the spot in left field where Mantle hit, the much-discussed homer, was pointed out to me. To tell the truth, I didn't believe it was possible. The distance from home plate to the bottom of the fence was 393 feet. There were ninety-four rows of bleachers, and ten feet above the last row of seats was a billboard twenty feet long and ten feet high. On top of the billboard was a clock eight foot long and eight foot high. Mantle hit the ball directly over the clock. I don't believe that I ever entered Griffith Stadium without looking at that spot and wondering how a baseball could be hit that far. In 1953, he went on to post an 11-8 record with a 3.29 average, pretty good numbers for a club that finished in seventh place.

By 1956, the twinkling star had become the ace of the staff and registered fifteen wins for the seventh place Senators. However, in 1957, he had the misfortune of losing his first 11 games. On June 21st, Calvin Griffith sponsored a "Break the Jinx Night." Fans were urged to bring their good luck charms to the park, and every fan was given a rabbit's foot as he entered the ballpark. Stobbs uniform number was changed to 13 and as he took the mound, the fans chanted and shook their good luck pieces. It worked! Stobbs and the Senators won the game.

In 1959, he pitched in the bullpen alongside of me and had a great ERA of 2.98, but his record ended up being 1-8 because he didn't get any run support when he was called upon to pitch.

Chuck played 15 years in the big leagues. He won 107 games, lost 130, and had a 4.29 career earned run average. He may have posted a winning record had he been on a team other than the Senators.

Al Worthington, Pitcher

My list of pitchers would not be complete without including Al Worthington. He arrived on the major league scene with the New York Giants in 1953. If my memory serves me correctly, he won his first two starts. He went on to win 32 games for the Giants in the next six years. In 1960 he was traded twice, first to the Red Sox and then to the White Sox. I guess it would be fair to say that Al, like so many of us who came to the majors in the early 1950s, had a difficult time handling all the hype and attention that constantly seemed to surround promising young, athletes. Choices were made, and sadly enough, not all of them

Chuck Stobbs

Ted Williams: 'Hey kid, just get it over the plate!'

Al Worthington

were the right ones.

He was raised in a Christian home and attended church, but his focus was on the world and its values. It happens a lot to people. In 1958, a dynamic change occurred in his life that could best be identified as a religious experience. He simply explained it this way, "I was saved at a Billy Graham Crusade."

When the White Sox traveled to Boston, we stayed at the Kenmore Hotel not far from Fenway Park. One day following the game, Al and I met in the hotel lobby and entered into a long conversation about religion in general and our beliefs in particular. A month later, the Red Sox traded him to the White Sox.

Worthington's beliefs were strong and he was always willing to testify to the strength of those convictions, but I don't ever remember his being forceful or turning anyone away. I was brought up in a religious home and raised to believe that Sunday was the Lord's Day. Dad didn't work on Sunday. My brothers and I were not allowed to play ball. No stores were open, but there was little or no money to spend.

These were the Depression days and Sunday afternoons were spent taking long walks and doing simple tasks around the house. My dad had to sign my first contract because I was under age. I remember him questioning the scout about me not having to pitch on Sunday. He assured my father that I would not be called upon to pitch on Sunday. So it was easy for me to understand Worthington's mind-set.

The White Sox were great at picking up signs. One day after a game, Worthington asked me, "Do you believe in cheating?"

"No!" I replied. The rumor was that the Sox were picking up the opponent's sign in an unacceptable manner.

"Russ, if you are truly a Christian, you will come with me to Al Lopez's office, and explain to him that we do not agree with these methods."

"No way," I responded. "First of all, it's most likely just baseball talk. Secondly, I'm lucky to be on this team, and I have the responsibility of caring for a wife and four children. If you express your beliefs to him and you're wrong, you'll be on your way to Indianapolis tomorrow."

He did and Lopez did! Al spent the next two seasons in the American Association at Indianapolis Indians.

Worthington played at Indianapolis for a year or so, then had a short stay in San Diego before going to Cincinnati in 1963. He developed into a good relief pitcher. In 1964, he was traded to Minnesota where he became a top closer for the Twins. He pitched in games four and seven of the 1965 World Series and in the American League Championship Series in 1969. He finished his career with the Twins in 1969. His career stats list a 3.39 ERA, 75 wins, 82 losses, and 110 saves in 14 seasons. He was also chosen as a member of the all-time Minnesota Twins team. What appeared in Chicago to be a career ending decision turned out to be a blessing that included a championship ring and a World Series appearance. The best years of his career were experienced after he stood firm on his Christian convictions.

The point of my story about Worthington is simply this. Everyone who has even the slightest knowledge of religious beliefs understands the necessity of having faith and trust in those beliefs, even though they run contrary to what people in the world think is right. Every religion has a Golden Rule, and every faith clearly stresses the importance of believing. In fact, the verb "believe," is an action verb that demands we take action. In the Old Testament, the book of Proverbs contains this verse: "Trust in the Lord with all your heart. Lean not to your own understanding, but in all ways acknowledge Him and He'll direct your path." It's a step of faith, regardless of what appears right or wrong to anyone else. I have often thought of Al's actions that day in Chicago. To the world, and to me at that time, his decision appeared foolish. But I find in the story of Job in the Old Testament that he would not turn from his God, even though he lost everything he possessed but in the end, his faith resulted in God restoring twice as much as he lost.

Nellie Fox, Infielder

Nellie Fox was Mr. Personality, Mr. Competitor and Mr. Nice Guy, all rolled into one. The day that Nelson Jacob Fox was elected into Baseball's Hall of Fame, every player that ever played with or against him bowed their heads to give God a moment of thanks, then lifted a mighty shout of joy that reached into the heavens because we were overjoyed that Nellie finally reached the goal he deserved.

Little Nel was what most of us who played the game would call a true competitor. He never gave an inch and always seemed to find a way to win with his bat, his glove or his intelligence. He never had the size of Mantle

Nellie Fox

or Maris, but what he lacked in size he made up for with heart, determination, hustle, and brains. Nellie understood the game of baseball. He also understood the mentality of those he played with and against. He studied the pitchers and knew what pitch to expect in any given situation. The pitching book on Fox called for pitchers to keep the ball down and inside so that he would pull the ball and keep it on the ground. If you pitched Nellie high he was trouble, because he could punch the ball over the infield or drop a bunt down the third base line.

Defensively, he used the same knowledge to size up the situation, hitter, and his pitcher. As a result he got a great jump on the ball and usually turned a base hit into a routine out. He seemed to always find a way to pick up his team. No wonder he was the league's MVP in 1959. His record-breaking streak of 798 games for second basemen ended on September 4, 1960, when illness kept him out of the lineup for four games. He was chosen for the American League All- Star Team ten successive years.

Fox was a punch hitter. The majority of his 2,367 career hits were singles (1,865). He also hit 355 doubles, 112 triples, and 35 home runs. He always seemed to find a way to get on base and put pressure on the defense to come up with great pitching or a great play to save the game. The Sox did not have a great deal of long ball power, but relied on finding a way to get on base or get into position to win a game. Pitchers in the league were always under pressure with Nellie at bat and a man on base in a tie or one run game. It was close to impossible to strike Nellie out. He led the league 10 times in the category of fewest strikeouts. In his 19 years in the league, Fox struck out only 216 times, an average of 11.4 times a year.

Personally, Nellie was a fantastic teammate and friend. I can't ever remember him being in a bad mood. He loved playing the game and the men he played with and against. He played the game the only way he knew how to play, giving 100 percent all the time. I don't believe he even knew the meaning of pressure or experienced stress. The greatest example of his composure that comes to mind took place in Baltimore in the latter half of the 1960 season. We were trailing the Yankees by a few games and at this point of the season each game took on more importance. A headline, in the Baltimore paper, speculated that Minnie Minoso and I were being considered in a trade with the Orioles. We were playing a twilight double-header and surprisingly, manager Al Lopez told me I was starting the first game, which somehow gave a little more credibility to the possibility of a trade. Minnie was upset by the news because he loved Chicago and didn't want to be traded. In the bottom of the first, there were two outs and a man on first. The next hitter, Clint Courtney, lifted an easy fly ball to left field, and I, assumed it was an easy third out, so I headed for the dugout. Somehow, Minnie lost the ball in the late afternoon sun. With two outs, the runner on first was off and running the moment the ball was hit. Lopez demanded that his pitchers back up the bases. I knew the runner on first would score, so I headed down the third base line to back up third base in the event the batter who hit the ball headed for third. Minoso, for some reason, threw the ball directly behind third base toward the Baltimore dugout. I was expecting the throw to be more between home plate and third and was not in position to track it down before the runner scored. I retired the next batter for the third out and went into the dugout. Lopez was all over me for not being in position to field the errant throw that allowed the second run to score. I tried to explain my reason for being were I was and that only made matters worse. Lopez screamed his displeasure and threw me out of the game. I walked dejectedly up the runway to the dressing room. I was upset. I threw off my shoes, slammed my glove into my locker and sat down to cool off. The television was on in the locker room, and it was apparent that we had a rally going in our half of the second inning. Suddenly, Nellie ran into the dressing room. He said, "What are you doing?"

I explained that Al had thrown me out of the game for not backing up the bases. "No", he said, "He's looking for you to bunt because he doesn't want to use a pinch hitter. You better get out there fast." I grabbed my shoes, struggled to put them on as I hurried down the runway to the dugout. I went straight to the bat rack and selected a bat, pulled on a batting helmet and sat on the bench.

Lopez looked around and saw me. "What the hell are you doing?" I'm going to bunt I replied.

"You are like hell. Get out of here before I take some of your money!"

I started toward the runway and there was Nellie and a couple of guys just laughing their heads off. I looked at Nellie and said. "You little SOB, if he takes my money, I'm going to break your neck!"

Long after that evening I thought about that game and what Nellie did.

Hey, the team knew it wasn't my fault that Minnie lost the ball in the twilight, but they were upset that Lopez took it out on me. Sometimes something like this pulls a team down. Nel did what he had to do to ease the tension. We ended up winning the game. I was not fined, and no trade took place.

They said Nellie would do anything to win and I believe it. By the way, I did get even with Fox at spring training the next year. I went fishing one evening and caught a large fish. If my memory serves me correctly, it was a small shark. With the help of a couple of guys, we managed to get into Nellie's room, short sheeted him, unscrewed the light bulbs, and put the fish in his bed. About 11 p.m. a terrifying scream came from Nellie's room. One might surmise that the devil himself was paying Nellie a visit. Once the screaming quieted down, a long, loud burst of profane language echoed through the hallways, along with a great deal of laughter. Gotcha Nellie!

He played in the major leagues for 19 years. He began his big league career with the Philadelphia Athletics in the American League in 1947. At the conclusion of the 1949 season, he was traded to the Chicago White Sox where he spent the next 13 seasons. He was sold to Houston of the National League in 1964 and completed his career in Texas the following season.

Luis Aparicio, Shortstop

When you speak of Nellie Fox, the name of Luis Aparico simultaneously leaps into your mind. For those of us, especially pitchers, that had the advantage of having both of them play behind us, they are inseparable. Like two peas in a pod would not be totally inaccurate. Statistically, they were relatively close. Each played in the majors about 18 years, and each played with the White Sox the major part of his career. Both thrived on getting on base any way possible. They were close in total number of hits, singles, doubles, triples and home runs. Luis hit more home runs than Nel, but Nellie hit more triples. In fact, Nellie led the league in that category several times.

The major similarities between them is amazing. Both are members of the Hall of Fame. Both great defensive players. Both would beat you with the bat, glove, or intelligence. And both were extremely productive in pressure situations.

Luis Aparicio

In Washington, the infield had trouble turning a double play. Pitchers are trained to pitch low with men on base because low pitching results in more ground balls. With the Senators, we often went against that rule and went for a strikeout or fly ball to get out of a difficult inning. With the White Sox we wanted the ground ball, because the double play was always a better choice than bearing down to get a strikeout. Luis had the better throwing arm, and Lopez took advantage of this by having Looie take all the cutoff throws from the outfield with men on base or in scoring position. Nellie would always cover the second base bag. The normal procedure was for the second baseman to receive all throws on balls hit to right or center field, and he shortstop take all throws from left and left center field. This little maneuver resulted in more than a few base runners being thrown out at third or home.

Aparcio had more range at short than anyone I had see with the exception of Ozzie Smith, and they were close. Luis not only had the range in both directions, he had the agility and athletic ability necessary to turn his body and get his arm into position to make a strong accurate throw. It is essential that every great shortstop be blessed with this ability. If not, chances are he will be moved to third or second base where a strong arm is less essential and the range from left to right more limited.

His speed at short was also used on the bases. He led the American League in stolen bases for nine consecutive years. He swiped 506 bases during his career. Luis believed in keeping a book on pitchers in regard to how big a lead you could take and what pitch were they most likely to throw in a given situation. He also listed the catcher's tendencies.

Looie, had a great personality and always seemed to have a smile on his face. He also got along well with teammates and always gave 100 percent all the time. When I joined the White Sox, I told Luis that I really liked Spanish food and I ended up eating a lot of meals with him.

Aparicio was voted into Baseball's Hall of Fame in 1984. He played 18 years in the major leagues. He had 2,677 hits and his lifetime batting average was .262. More importantly, he turned 1,556 double plays and had a fielding percentage of .972.

Harry Agganis, First base

Harry Agganis was a twinkling star that burned out well before his time for health reasons. He was one of the most talented athletes, among a multitude of great athletes I was fortunate to have played with during my career. He was an All-American quarterback and outstanding baseball player at Boston College.

He picked up the nickname "Golden Greek" because of his Greek-like body. Harry was one of the better-built athletes I have ever seen at six-foot-two and 200 pounds. His body compared with any of the Greek gods one might see in a museum or photograph. His muscles actually rippled as he walked, and his smile featured perfect white teeth and a broad mouth that lit up any room he entered. All of this coupled with a great personality and tremendous popularity, made him a favorite with his teammates and fans, especially the ladies. Agganis signed a bonus contract with Boston, and I believe the New England fans would have boycotted Fenway Park if the Red Sox had permitted him to sign with any other team.

I first met the Golden Greek in 1953 when he was assigned to Louisville, Boston's top farm team in the American Association. He was a hit with the team the moment he walked into the clubhouse. His personality and awesome smile drew you to him the minute you were introduced. His power, fluid movements, and strong throwing arm instantly impressed you with his baseball potential. More often than not, a new player must earn the respect of his teammates before he is accepted, but Harry won us over the first time he put on the uniform and stepped onto the field for practice.

Harry's first season in professional baseball was impressive. He had the same difficulty most players have making the transition from college baseball to the pros — the high level of play and the aggressive power of the pitching. He would go 2- for-4 against good pitching and 0-for-4 against super prospects on their way to the majors, or the crafty veteran that had been in the majors and was working for a last shot at the big leagues. Considering that Harry came right out of the college ranks and into AAA baseball his first season, his numbers were impressive. He played in 155 games for Louisville, went to bat 595 times, hit .281 with 108 RBI and 23 home runs. The future certainly looked bright for the Golden Greek.

When spring training camp opened for the Red Sox in Sarasota, Florida in 1954, his name was penciled into the lineup at first base for the

Red Sox. Agganis played in 132 games for Boston that season hitting .251 with 57 RBI's and 11 home runs. Certainly not Rookie of the Year numbers, but oh how encouraging! The Red Sox finally found the first baseman they had been looking to fill that slot in the infield for many years, and the loyal Red Sox fans were delighted to have one of their own, from Lynn, Massachusetts.

The 1955 season beamed with expectations for Agganis and the Red Sox, but it proved to be a disaster for both. The Golden Greek was experiencing some physical difficulty as spring training opened for the Sox. His energy level was down and he was having difficulty swinging the bat with authority. His power seemed short circuited, and he had difficulty reaching the outfield wall during batting practice. Once the season started things looked better for Harry. After 25 games, he was hitting .313, but only hit one home run. Then in the early part of June we were told that he had been rushed to the hospital, and a few days later on June 27, 1955, he passed away. I never learned what caused his death at the time, but his loss was tragic to the family, team, and baseball. According to his biography, he died from a blood clot to his lung that caused a pulmonary embolism. He had been diagnosed with pneumonia and phlebitis in his calf.

Bernie Allen, Infielder

Bernie Allen is one of many great athletes from the state of Ohio. He was born in the town of East Liverpool. Allen came from a section of Ohio that is prime ground for scouts seeking out football and baseball prospects. Bernie was both. Following graduation from East Liverpool High School, he accepted a full scholarship to Purdue University.

Allen quickly established himself on the gridiron as an outstanding Big Ten quarterback and a talented infielder on the baseball diamond. He led the Boilermakers to a few Big Ten upsets in football, knocking Ohio State, Minnesota, and Michigan State out of the Rose Bowl during his career. He was a unanimous All Big Ten player in both sports. He surprised many people when he signed a professional baseball contract rather than waiting to be selected in the football draft. Actually, Bernie said he received lots of interest from various teams prior to the football draft, but suggested they save the draft pick because he was going into baseball. In the late Fifties, football was just beginning to enter into its glory days therefore the

170

Harry Agganis

Bernie Allen

longevity offered in baseball was far more appealing than the bumps and bangs of football.

Following the football draft, Bernie did receive a visit from one of the owners of the Boston Patriots (now New England), trying to get him to reconsider and sign a football contract. That part owner of the Patriots was an impressive baseball celebrity in Boston, whose name just happened to be Dom DiMaggio of Boston Red Sox fame. Bernie was thrilled DiMaggio thought enough of him to personally seek him out, but it didn't change his mind. Bernie still decided to turn to baseball.

Calvin Griffith invited Allen to work out with the Senators in 1959 and saw enough potential to offer him a bonus in 1960 and launch him on his baseball career. Bernie had a good enough year at Charlotte to be invited to spring training with the Senators the following year. He got to know Billy Martin who he considers to be one of the most knowledgeable minds in baseball. More than that, he was also a great teacher. Having the knowledge and being able to teach it to others is a great talent. "I learned more baseball from Billy Martin in a short season than I did in my whole 12-year career," he explained.

Allen recalled a time when Martin was frank with a young fielder: "We were at spring training and we had a young infielder playing second base. There was a hard, but playable ball, hit at the kid. It was just a little too much for him to handle and he booted the ball. After the inning was over Bernie moved to the young player to encourage him and to point out his mistake. The kid felt bad about booting the ball, but before Bernie could reach the kid, Martin got to him first. Martin put his arm around the youngster and said, "Don't worry about that one don't be blaming yourself. It's not your fault, you don't belong in the big leagues anyway." Martin was released by the Twins and replaced at second base by Allen.

Allen was playing for the Washington Senators when Ted Williams was the manager. Ted had his theory on pitching, fielding, and of course hitting. Players in this and previous generations of baseball players did not have the luxury of lifting weights, playing other sports, or just enjoying an afternoon off, on the golf course. Williams had one rule not written into the player's contracts, but enforced — no golf! In fact, if you were caught golfing you were fined $1,000. That was a lot of money in those days, about a month's salary for most players. His theory was that golf would ruin your baseball swing. Bernie was a good golfer and enjoyed the game a great deal. One day he approached Ted and said, "Look, golf relaxes me and it won't change my baseball swing in any way."

"How come?" asked Williams.

Bernie replied, "Because I bat left handed and play golf right handed."

Williams said," That's the stupidest thing I ever heard. Why would you do a thing like that?"

In his exasperation, Allen responded, "So I don't ruin my golf swing!"

One evening several retired players were sitting around gabbing about the good old days, when the subject of pitching inside or brushing a hitter back was brought up. In our playing days being knocked down following a home run was as common in baseball as hot dogs and mustard. Bernie Allen explained, "When I played for the Senators, I followed Frank Howard to the plate. Hondo led the league in home runs in 1968 and in 1970. Let me tell you, I spent a lot of time on my back, and I expected and accepted it as one of the unwritten rules of the game.

Pitchers protected their right to the plate, and they certainly protected their teammates. Sal Maglie wasn't called the "Barber," because he cut hair in the off-season, and any pitcher worth his salt in those days pitched inside.

Allen spent a dozen seasons in the majors most of it in the American League with Washington, later the Twins, and Yankees. He had a brief stay with Montreal in the National League during his final season in 1973. Bernie, like so many of the Twinkling Stars, had great athletic ability. What destined him to the Twinkling Star category was simply not being in the right place at the right time. In 1972 he was with the Yankees. Sadly enough for Bernie that was one of the few years the Bronx Bombers didn't make it to the World Series, but they made it in 1973 when Bernie was with them for the first 17 games before being traded to the Expos. Being in the right place at the right time has a lot to do with success.

In 1999, the twinkling star was elected into the Purdue Athletic Hall of Fame.

Rocky Bridges, Infielder

Many baseball experts believe that pitching is about 70 percent of the game and great pitching will stop good hitting. However, one cannot overlook the value of outstanding infield play that can take, what appears to be a sure hit away from the hitter in a turn of a

Rocky Bridges

glove, or turns a hard hit ball into a classy double play. Those "grounder rooters" are the pitchers heroes.

Whenever I think of infielders, the name Rocky Bridges is the first name that leaps into mind. His given name was Everett Lamar Bridges and he was as tough a competitor as ever left the town of Refugio, Texas. He was also one of the most naturally, funny men I have ever been around. Besides all this he was a talented baseball player.

Rocky was a victim of the baseball system of the late Forties and Fifties. With only 16 teams in baseball, only four hundred positions were available in the majors. Teams could sign 40 players to major league contracts, but could only carry 25 on the rooster at one time, except for a brief period at the opening and closing of the season. It was customary for teams to carry nine or ten pitchers, which left fifteen positions to be divided among infielders, outfielders, and catchers. Baseball owners in those times were far less inclined to consider selling or trading talented players. Free agency was yet to be born, thus it was easy to get lost behind a Supernova or a talented minor league player and never even get a shot at making the big time. Baseball organizations had as many as thirty minor league teams in various levels of talent, ranging from the bottom of the ladder D leagues, and graduating from there to C, B, A, AA, and AAA. It was very easy to get lost. That, to some degree, was Rocky's misfortune.

He signed with the Brooklyn Dodgers and got lost behind a future Hall of Fame Supernova shortstop by the name of Pee Wee Reese. When the Dodgers finally did trade him after seven years in their organization, it was to the Cincinnati Reds. Once again, he had to battle with a pretty good shortstop, Roy McMillan, reputed to be the best in the National League. Rocky's next stop was the talent hungry Washington Senators, who were willing to grasp at any straw to gain a little respectability. On May 20, 1957, he became a Senator. The fact that Bridge's career fielding percentage was a very respectable .969 is a strong indicator that he could "pick it," but at this point in his career, he had lost a step or two. One asset that never diminished was a fantastic sense of humor that kept the team loose and laughing regardless of the folly that often appeared in our play.

Everett Lamar Bridges was five-foot-ten inches and tipped the scale at 175. He was bow legged, which was most likely the result of spending a great deal of time on horseback growing up in Refugio, Texas. He also liked to chew tobacco, not just an average plug, but an overflowing jaw full. To top this off, he had a uncharacteristic high-pitched voice. The first time I stepped onto the mound with Rocky at short and heard his ringing tones of encouragement coming from the shortstop position, I remember a deadly silence hovering over the stadium as the high tones vibrated across the infield. "C'mon, Russ baby. Get em' out, kid!" If I were to choose a cartoon character that would best give you the best description of his appearance, Popeye would be the one. The only difference being that Popeye held a pipe in his teeth and Rocky held a chew in his jaw.

One night we were playing the Yankees at Griffith Stadium. Rain prior to the game made the infield and outfield grass slippery. When the game got underway, Elston Howard was at bat for the Yankees with two out and the bases empty. He lined a low fastball directly toward Bridges at short. The ball never rose higher than a few inches above the turf and skipped off the wet surface like a bullet. Rocky was set to field the ball, but he never had a chance to get his glove into position. It hit him in the forehead! He dropped as if he had been shot! Players from both teams rushed out onto the field. Our trainer George Lentz broke through the crowd of players and turned Rocky onto his back. He did the standard thing for trainers in those days, called his name, held up three fingers, then asked the question, "Rocky, are you okay? How many fingers am I holding up?"

The tobacco chewing burly shortstop replied in his high-pitched voice, "Doc, you don't think this is going to ruin my chances of me getting in the movies, do you?" The players around him burst into laughter. We were laughing so hard we didn't even realize that players from both teams were leaning all over each other. The ball, which originally appeared to hit Rocky directly in the head, had in reality, glanced off the side of his cheek and slid into his shirt through the neck opening. This added to the mystery of the whereabouts of the ball. Someone had suggested he had swallowed his chaw and it was actually the ball that was lodged in his cheek. It was one of the most humorous things I have ever heard happening in a major league game. I have often wondered what the 30,000 fans must have thought.

Later in the season, we were in New York. I had to hustle to make the team bus to the stadium and missed breakfast. I was out in the bullpen for this series, and along about the third inning, I became hungry. I took a baseball out of the ball bag, went behind the fence to the bullpen, and approached a young fan standing by the gate. "Hey, kid!" I said, "If you go get me a hot dog, I'll give you this ball and sign it for you."

The kid took off like a shot and soon returned with this beautiful New York hot dog with the works: mustard, pickle, and onion. I returned to the bullpen just in time to hear the phone ring. Chuck Stobbs, our starting pitcher, was in trouble and they were calling to get me ready to go into the game if it became necessary. I folded the hot dog in the wrapper and placed it in my pitching jacket pocket. As fate would have it, Stobbs didn't get out of trouble. A few minutes later, I was walking from the left field bullpen to the mound in Yankee Stadium with this hot dog in my glove. I had moved it from my pocket because I was afraid that it would fall out onto the field. When I arrived at the mound, I was greeted by Rocky. Our manager, Cookie Lavagetto, was at home plate talking to the umpire as he made the lineup changes. I turned to Rocky and said, "What am I going to do with this hot dog?" "Give it to me," he said, and slipped it into his back pocket. Lavagetto joined us on the mound, handed me the ball and said, "Dutch you got the bases loaded, no one out, and Mantle, Berra, and Skowron coming up. Go get 'em."

Before either of us could move, Rocky handed Cookie the hot dog and said "Here, skipper, keep it warm, he'll be in for it in a minute." Lavagetto just shook his head and walked to the dugout. As it turned out, it was the highlight of the day. Mantle struck out, Yogi popped to the catcher behind home plate, and Moose flied to center. When I entered the dugout, Cookie handed me the hot dog and said, "Here you deserve this."

Bridges career covered 11 seasons. His batting average was .247. He was another of the many twinking starts who was never quite in the right place at the right time to take advantage of his talent. But he was a great guy, a fantastic teammate, and a hell of a competitor.

Billy Consolo, Infielder

S peaking of being in the right place at the right time helps me to introduce my next infielder, Billy Consolo. Billy was one of the bonus babies of the early fifties. The rule in baseball in those days stated that any player signed for a bonus exceeding $6,000 had to remain with the major league team for a minimum of two years. Consolo came under this rule when he signed with the Red Sox for a bonus listed at $100,000.

Consolo had all the tools; he was big, strong, and mature for his age.

Billy Consolo

Sammy Esposito

He had the quickness, range, and a fantastic arm, all of which projected him as a big league infielder. Billy, like most young players, could swing the bat, but hitting high school pitching and being able to hit a major league pitching everyday, especially the breaking ball, is a different story, nor does it take into consideration the defensive range of the major league infielders and outfielders that turn well-hit balls into routine outs. As a result Billy went to bat only 65 times for the Red Sox in 1953, hitting .215. He had fourteen hits, two base on balls, and twenty- three strikeouts. The following year he played in 91 games went to bat 242 times, recorded 55 hits, 33 base on balls, but once again his 69 strikeouts was more than his hit total. It was not until his fifth season that his numbers moved into the respectable range. In 1957 he hit .270 in 68 games for the Red Sox.

I believe that Consolo had all the physical ability to be an outstanding major league baseball player, maybe even a Hall of Fame caliber player. Maybe, just maybe the signing bonus and not getting the experience in the minor leagues kept him from baseball glory. Who knows?

Consolo spent ten years in the major leagues with six teams: Red Sox, Senators, Twins, Angels, Royals and Phillies.

Sammy Esposito, Infielder

Sammy Esposito is a prime example of being in the wrong place at the wrong time, which had a definite bearing on the total numbers he was credited with during his career. Sammy was a homegrown product who made his first bid for athletic fame at Fenger High School in Chicago, Illinois. From there, he moved onto Indiana University were he built a solid reputation, earning All Big Ten honor's in basketball and baseball. Then he went straight to the Chicago White Sox.

Esposito was one of the best, if not the best, utility infielders in base-ball. The fact that he stayed with one team the majority of his career gives a strong indication that he had all the tools necessary to play the game at the major league level. The White Sox had numerous offers to trade or sell Sammy, but they knew his value to the team and rejected all such offers. He could have started for most of the teams in either league. I have no doubt he could have started at second or short for the Senators. His ability to play third, second or shortstop made him unique. Sam's quickness of foot made him a valuable pitch-runner, and his ability to handle the bat in a bunting situation or hitting behind the runner, made him an even greater asset. I'm positive that Sammy enjoyed every moment of his ten years in the major leagues, but I'm certain he would have liked to have the opportunity of seeing what he could do in a regular lineup.

Unless you have great knowledge or have played the game, it is impossible to realize how difficult it is to sit on the bench day after day and suddenly be thrown into the heat of a ball game and expect to excel, especially at bat. Esposito's batting average at Waterloo, .265 in 1953, and Memphis, .281 in 1955, give a good indication that Sam could hit when he was in the regular lineup. He spent 1954 in the military service.

What numbers Sammy would have put up under different circumstances, we will never know, but playing beside two future Hall of Fame players in Fox and Aparicio didn't enhance his chances. He was another of those perfect fit guys with the White Sox. He fit perfectly with the rest of the guys that I believe made up the most compatible club in baseball. Sammy was traded to Kansas City in 1963. After baseball, he coach the sport for many seasons at the University of South Carolina.

Billy Klaus, Infielder

I first met Billy Klaus when he played in the American Association with Toledo and Milwaukee. I got to know him a little better when we were teammates for a short period with Boston when he joined them in 1955. Billy was another of the Twinkling Stars that had a long career in the major leagues with both Boston teams, the Braves and the Red Sox. Billy also played with Baltimore and Washington in the American League and Milwaukee and Philadelphia in the National League.

He was a super infielder with a great bat and difficult to strike out with enough power to put one in the seats. He hit ten home runs with the Red Sox in 1957. Quickness, speed, a great glove, a good arm, and the ability to play second, short and third made him a valuable asset for any major league team. He hit .283 for the Red Sox in 1957, which proved he could contribute if he had the opportunity to play every day. His career covered eleven years. He had a career batting average of .249. He hit 40 home runs, and had a .956 fielding average.

In February of 2002, I saw Billy at the Ted Williams Museum. A group of us were having dinner together. Many people from the community were attending the dinner as fund-raisers and the former players were more than happy to sign baseballs to be sold off to the highest bidders. One of these

Billy Klaus

Ted Williams: 'Hey kid, just get it over the plate!'

Pete Runnels

ladies was so excited because she heard Billy and his wife speaking about Billy's painting. She thought Billy had donated a painting for the auction. She turned to Billy and said, "Mr. Klaus, do you do oil's or watercolors?"

"Houses!" the former player and painter replied with a smile.

"Oh!" she replied in surprise.

Pete Runnels, Infielder

Pete Runnels was one of the most versatile twinkling star infielders I ever played with. He had to be one of the best-liked players in the American League. He always had a smile on his face that lit up the ballpark. He always appeared happy, relaxed, and totally content with his family, friends, and the game he loved. "Pistol Pete," as he was nick-named, was one of those good old Texas boys who took things in stride without being bent out of shape. His philosophy was, "Well, the sun don't shine on the same dogs ass everyday so you might just as well make the best of what comes your way."

He was one of what I call, the true infielder. He could play second, third, short, or first with equal ease and efficiency; although he was better equipped more as a middle infielder than at first or third. Many years, he played all four positions in a season.

Any major league infielder will tell you that it is easier to play one position everyday than it is to switch from one to another. For example, when playing third base the ball gets to you faster than it does at short or second, so you have a little more time to judge the speed of the ball and move into position to make the play. With all the changing of positions that Pete did in his career, his fielding average was never lower than .949, and he averaged less than 13 errors a season. The figures are remarkable when you consider that he handled over 250 chances a season.

On the offensive side of the game, Pete was the kind of hitter pitchers hate to pitch to because he always seemed to get wood on the ball, and he didn't swing at bad pitches. He was difficult to strike out, averaging below 40 strikeouts a season. Runnels also chalked up 60 walks a year to go along with a lifetime batting average of .291.

To say that Pistol Pete was a tough out would not be overstating his ability. He won two batting titles during his career: in 1960 hitting .320 and again in 1962 when he hit .326. I might also add that he hit .322 in 1958, but was edged out by a teammate. Runnels batted second in the lineup, Ted Williams hit third. Going into the last day of the season Pete was leading Ted by a few percentage points. Boston and Washington were scheduled to play a season ending double-header at Griffith Stadium. When the first game ended Ted had pulled ahead of Pete by a couple of points. He could have sat out the second game of the double-header and forced Runnels to go at least 3-4 in order to win the title, but Ted declined Manager Pinky Higgins offer to sit out the second game.

The catch in the story comes about in the second game when Runnels drilled a long drive into the gap in right center that was a sure stand-up double and perhaps a triple. But for some unknown reason Pete pulled up at first base. Most of the fans and players alike assumed that Pete had pulled a muscle. When he was approached following the game for an explanation, Runnels remarked, "If I had gone to second, I would have left first open and they would have walked Ted. With me at first, it forced them to pitch to him, and I wanted to give him the opportunity to hit." It was a far more emotional situation than most of the fans and media realized, but it certainly pointed out the quality and character of Runnels.

Pete's career covered fourteen seasons with three teams, the Washington Senators, Boston Red Sox, and Houston Astros. Runnels lifetime batting average was .291. During his career, he punched out 1,854 hits, and had a fielding average of .982.

Roy Sievers, First Base/Outfielder

I had the pleasure of being a teammate of Roy Sievers for five seasons, three with the Washington Senators and two more with the Chicago White Sox. Sievers picked up the nicknamed of "Squirrel" because the close set of his eyes and the roundness of his cheeks gives him the appearance of a squirrel.

Roy is another example of a superb twinkling star who had a long major league career of 17 seasons. He never quite received the attention from the media that his talent justified. Ted Williams called his swing, "the sweetest swing in baseball." It was short, powerful, and consistent. The shortness allowed him to wait until the very last second to make a decision on the pitch and still rip at it with power. The consistency of the swing made it difficult to fool him with a breaking ball or an off speed pitch.

Perhaps the best example of fate having to do with what a players final

Roy Sievers

numbers will be, and how he is perceived by baseball is the 1957 season. Roy led the league with 42 home runs and 114 RBI. He also managed to hit .301 with the Washington Senators, who struggled to win 55 games while losing 99. I have heard the argument that since Roy was with a last-place team, opposing pitchers threw to him rather than around him. I maintain just the opposite was true. It would be easier to pitch around him because the only other power hitter in the Senator's lineup was Jim Lemon, who hit 17 home runs. Pitchers are not known for our sympathy when it comes to getting hitters out. Winning games is what it's all about! If pitching around a hitter was the difference between wining or losing a game I would pitch around him, regardless of what place the club held in the standings.

Roy had a fantastic year in 1957, but so did a couple of other darn good hitters by the name of Williams and Mantle. Williams led the American with a .388 batting average, which was remarkable since he 39 years old and nearing the end of his career. He hit 38 home runs and drove in 87 runs. Mantle hit a lofty .365 with 34 homers and 94 RBI. Williams and Sievers led the league in slugging percentage .731. Roy hit 42 home runs and RBI leader with 114. Williams won his fifth batting title, but it was Mantle who was named the MVP. You don't have to be a genius to figure out who received the media's accolades. My point here is not to minimize the great numbers that Ted and Mickey put on the board, or to chastise the media for not giving Sievers more print, but to emphasize once again that Roy's accomplishments were lost in the brightness of two Supernovae. Another time, another place, a different team, or perhaps more average numbers by other players would have cast Sievers into the limelight.

An ironic twist that took place following the 1957 season. No multi-year contracts existed in those days. Everything was based on one year at a time. Raises or cuts in the new contract depended upon several things: the amount of profit the team made, where the team finished in the standings, and your personal statistics, which included every part of the game. In order to get any sizable increase it was necessary to put up impressive numbers in almost every category. You may have had a great year hitting but if your fielding percentage was down or you were lacking in some area of play, you could expect some deduction from your contract.

Roy tells the story of receiving his 1958 contract from Calvin Griffith with a little more than average concern. It seems that Calvin had forgotten that Roy hit .301, and led the league in home runs, and RBI. He opened the contract with great anticipation, expecting a sizable raise in salary, but much to his surprise the contract called for a $10,000 cut in pay. Roy leaped for the phone, and upon reaching Calvin, explained that there was a mistake. The person who typed the contract must have deducted the 10,000 instead of adding it to the contract. Mr. Griffin quietly explained that there had not been a mistake. After all, the club finished last in the league, had won only 55 games, and attendance was down from the previous season. Therefore, a pay cut was in order. Roy quickly pointed out his league leading numbers. Clark's reply was, "You better sign it because if you can ring up those numbers and the team still finishes last who did they benefit? We can finish last with you or without you." Sievers held out and finally settled for a $4,000 raise.

His career covered 17 seasons, mostly in the American League with Washington and Chicago. He did play a couple of seasons in the National League with the Phillies in 1962 and 1963. Roy played on either last-place or low-standing teams in 13 of his 17 seasons. Most of his career was with the St Louis Browns and the Washington Senators. His four winning seasons were with the White Sox in 1960-61, and Philadelphia in 1962-63.

Sievers' career batting average was .267, and his lifetime fielding average was .989, which included play in the outfield and first base. He hit 318 home runs and had 1,147 RBI. He also was the 1949 Rookie of the Year in the American League. He was the only Washington Senator named to the 1956 American League All-Star Team.

Roy has more friends in and out of baseball than anyone I know. I have never heard of anyone who had anything negative to say about him. He was a great asset to the game of baseball. I am pleased to say that our friendship has continued over the years. We see each other several times a year at golf outings and we chat on the phone often.

Bill Skowron, First Base

Bill Skowron and I broke into baseball in the Class C Piedmont League in 1951. Bill was with Norfolk, Virginia in the Yankee farm system, and I was with Roanoke, Virginia in the Red Sox system. "Moose" was born in Chicago, Illinois and was recruited by the Yankees out of Purdue University. His nickname gives a fairly good indication of his size and strength. He played a little football at Purdue,

Bill Skrowon

but his major interest was baseball.

The first time Roanoke traveled to Norfolk I was introduced to Bill in a way that I have never forgotten. To say the least, I was a real hot shot college pitcher at the University of Pittsburgh I average 15 strikeouts a game and I don't ever remember a right-handed hitter belting one of my curve balls out of the park to right field.

The second time I faced Bill in that game I threw him a curveball. It was a little up in the strike zone and he belted it over the right field fence about 330 feet. Bill was the first, but I am sure not the last, right-handed batter to accomplish this feat. I certainly learned something about pitching to Skowron, because I only gave up one home run to him the rest of my career, and that took place on May 10, 1958, in New York. Someone might ask, "How do you remember all that?"

"I don't, someone from SABR (Society for American Baseball Research) gave me a printed list of everyone who ever hit a home run off me during my career along with the date, location, inning and the score at the time it was hit," he explained.

Like most pitchers, I have a tendency to forget those sad moments, which is why I don't recall them. I do remember one solid line drive Skowron hit off me, but it turned out to be a time at bat and not a hit. I was with the White Sox at the time and we were playing the Yankees in New York. I had difficulty wearing a normal jock strap with a pocket because it rubbed against my leg and was uncomfortable. I found the best method for me was to use two jock straps and a pair of cut off shorts with the cup in between the two straps. This allowed the cup to move without rubbing in one spot. Bill hit a lined a shot right back to the mound. I sensed its location and my natural instinct to survive caused me to move my thighs together. This allowed the cup to be braced against my thighs, and when the ball hit my thighs absorbed the power of the line drive rather than the cup. The normal language used in baseball to describe getting hit in the groin was, "ringing the bell." When the ball hit it dropped straight down and rolled a foot or so toward home plate, I fielded it and threw Bill out at first. I believe both clubs were relieved that I was not seriously hurt and at the same time amazed at my non-reaction to the batted ball. The players on the White Sox asked where the ball hit and I explained what happened. In any event, I earned the nickname of "Num Nuts" for a few days. To tell the truth if it had hit me without my legs absorbing the force,

I might not be writing this story now.

One other story I want to relate about Moose goes back to 1952, when Bill was playing for the Yankee's Triple-A farm team in Kansas City. I'm pulling this out of memory and have not checked it out, but I believe Bill was voted the outstanding minor league baseball player of the year. If my memory serves me right, he set a record with 55 home runs, well over 100 RBI, and a batting average above .300. The most amazing thing about Skowron's year was that the Yankees didn't send him a major league contract the next year, and he played again at Kansas City. Today, if a player had that kind of season he would have been called up to the parent club after a month. He had another good year in 1953 and joined the Yankees in 1954 for his rookie season.

Ted Williams, Outfielder

Ted Williams was once asked, "How would you like to be remembered?" Without hesitation, he replied, "As the greatest hitter to ever play the game of baseball." Some would argue their case for Babe Ruth, Ty Cobb, Hank Aaron, Joe DiMaggio, Willie Mays, Stan Musial, or Barry Bonds. I cast my vote for Williams as the greatest hitter of all time based on my personal observation of playing with and against him. With Williams hitting was more than a God-given talent. It was his profession, avocation, vocation, chosen goal, and most of all his life! He once said that hitting a round ball traveling at 90 to 100 miles per hour squarely on a round bat was the most difficult thing to do in sports. It took concentration, determination, fantastic eyesight, and great eye-hand coordination, and Ted had them all.

One example of his great vision took place at spring training in Sarasota, Florida, following his second tour of military duty with the Marines. When Ted took his turn in the batting cage for the first time he complained, "What have they done to this field it's out of alignment?" His comment was taken with raised eyebrows and with more than a little shaking of heads. Williams was so insistent that a surveyor was brought in to set the left and right field lines. The results proved Ted was right on target, home plate was out of line and had to be reset.

Just for the sake of argument, let's look at his statistics. In his twenty-one year major league career, he only once hit below .300 and that was in 1959 at the age of 42. His batting average that year was .254. His batting

Ted Williams

average for his career was a lofty .344. He is the last man to hit 400. Actually, he did this twice. In 1941, he led the American League with a batting average of .406.

The fact that he was hitting .401 going into the final day of the season is well documented. The story of refusing manager Joe Cronin's offer to sit out the final day double-header to protect the .400 batting average is one of the games most memorable stories. His average would have been higher, but in 1941 there was no sacrifice fly rule. I can't find any records that list how many fly balls he hit that would have been recorded as sacrifice flies, but one thing is certain, his average would have been higher than .406. In 1953, the year he returned from military service, he hit .407, but only had 91 times at bat.

One might want to take into consideration his league leading average of .388 at age forty. Dick Collins, who for years was the photographer and public relations representative for the Baseball Hall of Fame in

Cooperstown put together some statistics based on the average number of times Williams would have gone to bat had he not given those years out of his career to serve his country as a Marine. Collins estimated that Ted would have gone to bat 787 times in the games he missed while serving his country. Those projected numbers would place Ted close to the top in the majority of batting categories. He would have ranked fourth in games played, eighth in total times at bat, first in runs scored, fourth in total hits, third in total home runs, first in total extra base hits, first in runs batted in, second in total bases, first in number of base on balls, and tied for first in grand slam home runs. The point I'm making is his unbelievable determination to be the best hitter to ever play got him just that, the games greatest hitter! Totals like these don't happen by accident, or simply by God-given talent, or by taking ones skills for granted. It takes the ultimate of self-discipline and daily commitment. Ted had a book on every pitcher he faced. It didn't matter if the pitcher were a rookie or a seasoned veteran, he asked questions of other players to find out what the guy had to offer and what he would throw in a tight situation.

I believe that Williams has to be included in a class of athletes, coaches, or leaders who stand a cut above the standard when it comes to focus, determination, concentration, and an all-out willingness to be the best. Being dedicated to reaching a goal, regardless of circumstances or detours, is not for the faint of heart. Those who believe that their way is the best approach to success and are willing to take exception with those who disagree stand tall in the rankings of success stories. The group I speak of would include names such as Vince Lombardi, Jackie Robinson, Bobby Knight, Bill Parcells, Michael Jordan, Chris Everett, Wilma Rudolph, Billy Jean King, and Lance Armstrong. These are overachievers!

I don't know a great deal about those who played baseball before I took an interest in the game except for the statistics listed beneath their names, but I do know that I would be hard pressed to change my opinion that Ted Williams is the greatest "Pure" hitter that has ever played the game of baseball.

In baseball that some hitters give their bats more attention than they sometimes do their wives. And some hitters on a hot streak would actually take the bat with them when they left the ballpark. No one was more particular about his bats than Ted Williams.

All bats in those days were Louisville Sluggers made by Hillerich and

Bradsby in Louisville, Kentucky. Jack Hillerich, who is currently the president of the company, told me a story about his father Bud and Williams. Ted often visited the plant just to pick out the wood for his bats. During one such trip just prior to the opening of spring training. He ordered a dozen bats. They were ready for shipment about the time Hillerich and his family was preparing to head for Florida. Hillerich, along with several of his top employees, visited every major league training camp every spring to talk with the players and sign top minor league prospects to a bat contract with his company. On this occasion, he delivered the bats Ted ordered personally. Ted inspected each bat, one by one looking at the grain and making sure the sweet spot was in the center of the hitting area. At one point during the inspection, he hesitated as he felt the bat, then laid it aside. After inspecting the remaining bats, he returned to the one he had laid aside. Picking it up, he handed it to Bud. "This one is a little heavy" William said.

Bud replied, "Okay, let's get a scale and see what it weighs." Sure enough, the bat was a half-ounce heavier than the others.

Another thing that players did to protect the bat from checking was to bone it. Checking occurs where the grain of the bat reaches the surface of the wood. As it dries, the bat has a tendency to peel or splinter slightly. To prevent this from happening and to harden the hitting surface players would bone the bat. The tool needed to bone a bat was a large hambone that had been cooked with the meat removed and dried. The bone was rubbed over the hitting surface of the bat again and again until the wood was hardened. In most cases, the job of boning a bat was passed on to the starting pitchers, who would not be playing between starting assignments. With little to do but cheer, the boning was done during the game. I had the honor of boning several bats for Williams. With the invention of aluminum bats use in Little League through college play players think I am kidding them about boning a bat.

The Splendid Splinter, which sports writers called him, achieved his lofty number by setting goals. Each time he came to bat his goal was to do his best, whether it was practice or a real game. Every hit was a step forward. Every out was a step back.

Williams led the American League in batting six times. I thought it was interesting to find the titles he won were always back-to-back: 1941-1942, 1947-48, and again in 1957-58. Mike Higgins, the Boston manager

195

knew that he had to give him a rest during the 1957 season to keep him strong. Ted was 40 years old and proper rest was essential. He responded with the second highest batting average of his career, .388. His 38 home runs were the second highest number in his career, only five short of the 43 he hit in 1949. The amazing thing was that with these numbers Ted didn't win the Most Valuable Player award. He didn't win the MVP award for several reasons. First, Mickey Mantle had an outstanding season and certainly the numbers he put up were worthy of MVP consideration. He hit .365 with 34 home runs and 94 runs batted in. Secondly, the Yankees won the American League pennant while Boston was never in contention. Finally, keep in mind the fact that Ted and the New York press were not exactly close, especially if it came to making a decision for the hometown team.

In 1958, Ted won his sixth batting title. The success he experienced the previous season had his confidence level at an all-time high. His numbers in home runs, batting average, runs scored, and runs batted in was down from the previous year, but the battle to win the title was far greater. In 1957, he won the race by .23 points over Mantle. That year his battle with Boston teammate Pete Runnels was a contest that went down to the last day of the season.

In 1959, Williams' average dipped to .254, the lowest of his career. He could have quit at this point, and many in the media and in baseball made that suggestion. Once again the character and quality of the man arose. He played one last season in 1960, hit 29 home runs, and finished the season with a .316 average. In his last plate appearance, Ted hit a home run off

Mickey Mantle

My son Rusty, Robin Sievers, Kevin and Peter Lollar got to meet Mickey Mantle at Comiskey Park one Sunday afternoon.

of Jack Fisher. It was the 521st of his career.

Mickey Mantle, Outfielder

Mickey Mantle was one of the greatest athletes to play the game of baseball. He had speed that allowed him to outrun balls hit in the left and right field gaps, turning them into routine plays. He had that sixth sense that permitted him to track well-hit balls the second it left the bat and arrive at the spot before the ball did. He had an outstanding arm, keeping runners from taking the extra base. His running time from home to first base or second was as good as anyone who ever played the game, and enabled him to beat out slow hit and hard to handle

197

balls and turn them into base hits.

Mickey's power from both sides of the plate made him one of the most feared hitters in the game. Many of his long home runs have been listed as the longest in baseball. I never entered Griffith Stadium without wondering how a ball could be hit as far as the home run he hit off of Chuck Stobbs. It was measured at 565 feet. Mickey hit five home runs off me during my career.

I remember another side of Mickey Mantle, a gentler, appreciative side. When I was with the White Sox, we had a family day a Comiskey Park on a Sunday afternoon and the Yankees were in town. My two sons — Russell Dean, named after Dizzy Dean, and my youngest, Darrel — had on their White Sox uniforms. Mick walked over to me and said, "You ought to be damn glad those boys look like their mother." Then he bent down and shook hands with Russell and kind of rubbed Darrel's head. It most likely didn't mean a great deal to the boys at the time they've probaby forgotten it. But I remember. It's hard to forget Mickey Mantle!

Roger Maris, Outfielder

Roger Maris, a teammate of Mickey Mantle with the Yankees, is another player I had a great deal of respect for in those days. Roger had a different life-style than Mickey. He was quiet, far less talkative and outspoken than Mantle, but someone you could talk to and who was always friendly.

Roger had power, but it was not in the same category as Mickey's. A lot of the fan mail I get ask the same question. "How many home runs did Roger hit off you in 1961? The answer is two. He hit number fifteen on June 4, 1961, at Comiskey Park in the top of the third inning with the bases empty. He hit his thirty-ninth in New York on July 25, 1961, in the fourth inning. Again the bases were empty.

In February of 2002, I had the pleasure of meeting Roger's family at the Ted Williams Museum. They were there to stand in for Roger to receive Ted's award for great accomplishment. Maris now being considered for the Baseball Hall of Fame by the Veterans Committee.

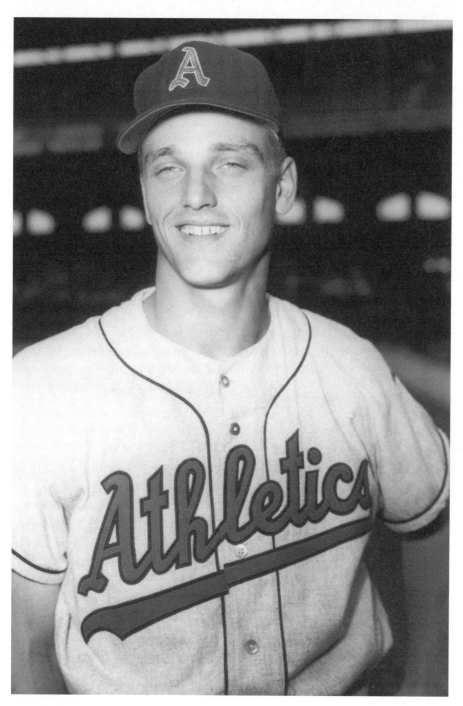

Roger Maris

Charlie Maxwell, Outfield

Charlie Maxwell is another one of my prime examples of a Twinkling Star. He was up and down from the minors to the big leagues more times that a bronco rider in a rodeo. Maxwell was a teammate of mine at Louisville when I first joined the team in 1952. By that time he had already had a couple of short trips to Boston. He was also on the roster with me in my rookie season at Boston.

Charlie picked up the nickname of "Smokey" because of his ability to really sting a baseball. He didn't swing hard, nor was he an impressive or imposing figure, but much like Ted Williams, he hit under the ball and it seemed to carry forever.

Smokey wore out Triple-A pitching because the majority of pitchers were not big league caliber. He would go 3-4 against these guys and 0-4 against the prospects.

One of Maxwell's problems was finding a position for him to play. He did not have the foot speed or arm strength to play the outfield. Since he was left-handed, the only option left was first base. He was adequate at this position but not golden glove material. As a result he bounced back and forth between the two positions and between the major and minor leagues.

The other problem that plagued Smokey was finding a team that was able to fit his skills to a position he could play. For example, in Boston with the short left field wall and his average arm and foot speed, left field was a perfect fit, but a fellow named Ted Williams was there. The Red Sox had Harry Agganis being groomed at first base, which left Maxwell drifting in the outfield.

Charlie finally got the break he needed when he was traded to Detroit. The Tigers had the short wall in right field, which was

Charlie Maxwell

200

perfect for the left-handed power-hitting Maxwell. He didn't have to cover a lot of ground in right field because he had Al Kaline or Harvey Kuenn, a former shortstop, patrolling centerfield.

Smokey finally found a home. For the next five years with the Tigers, he averaged better than 25 home runs a season. He finished his fourteen-year career with a batting average of .264 and 148 homers. He hit three of those home runs off me.

If you don't believe that being in the right place at the right time, and being fortunate enough to fit into the teams needs, take a closer look at Maxwell's career. That's what being a twinkling star is all about.

Jimmy Piersall, Outfielder

Jimmy Piersall was one of the best defensive outfielders in baseball, if not the strangest. He was a natural centerfielder but had the ability to play all three fields. Jim was chosen to take over the centerfield spot from Dom DiMaggio when the Little Professor decided to retire in 1953. Jim responded to the challenge by hitting a solid .272 in 585 times at bat. Defensively, his fielding percentage topped the scale at .987. He had 352 putouts, 15 assists and only five errors during the course of the season.

Jimmy Piersall

The Red Sox were counting on big things from Jimmy in 1954 and he lived up to those expectations by hitting .285 and again producing another outstanding fielding average of .985 with only four errors. During spring training in 1954, Jim's personality seemed to be changing. I roomed with him during spring training and he would get up every morning around 5 o'clock and go to church. Often he would not return to the room at night until after I had fallen asleep. Several times I felt my bed moving during the night and awoke to find Jim moving the bed. I'd ask him what he was doing and he'd reply, "I'm suppose to move it closer to the door."

His habits continued to border on the unusual, and by the time the club headed north for the opening of the season, his actions were getting worse. One of his more notable acts was to pull a water gun from his back pocket and squirt home plate as the umpire was tying to dust it with his whisk-broom. The act resulted in him being rejected. He continued to be thrown out of ballgames for silly stunts such as kicking dirt on home plate or hitting a pop fly to the infield and instead of running to first base he would run toward third.

Once when he was ejected from a game, he got dressed and sat in the left field stands and led the fans in a cheer for Jim Piersall. The club decided that he was on the verge of a nervous breakdown and had him evaluated. He missed twenty games, but returned to the team to complete the season. About this time in his career a biographical book he had written, *Fear Strikes Out*, was published. Later, the book was turned into a movie of the same name, starring Anthony Perkins. There was a genuine feeling of mixed feelings surrounding Jimmy's emotion, the book, and the movie. Some thought it was just hype, others didn't question the nervous breakdown. Most of the team didn't like the movie version of the book mainly because Anthony Perkins was about as athletic as a three-legged jackass. He couldn't run, swing a bat, and most of all, couldn't throw a baseball, but he was great in the weird scenes.

Jimmy was in right field on July 18, 1954, when I made my first start for the Red Sox that turned out to be a one-hit 4-0 shutout over Baltimore and Bob Turley. Piersall opened the fourth inning with a home run into the screen in left field to give us a 3-0 lead going into the fifth inning. Piersall may have been a bit unusual but he was a great asset to the team.

Piersall had a 17-year career in the major leagues with the Red Sox, Indians, Senators, Mets and Angels. Jimmy remained close to the game as a broadcaster with the Angels.

Jimmy had a lifetime batting average of .272 with 1,604 hits, 104 home runs, and an outstanding fielding percentage of .988.

Steve Korcheck, Catcher

Steve Korcheck is an outstanding example of players of this golden age, who had an opportunity to play in the majors, but had the intelligence to realize there is life after baseball. Steve was with the Senators about four years. He was a great receiver, good hands, good arm, and he stayed low in his crouch behind the plate. Most pitchers love to pitch to guys like Steve. Perhaps, like so many others, his career at a different time or place under different circumstances would have been better.

Steve's situation reminds me a great deal of the decision made by the doctor, played by Burt Lancaster, whose life-long ambition was to go to bat one time in the major leagues in *Field of Dreams*. He accomplished this thanks to Kevin Costner and James Earl Jones, who tracked him down and took him to the field of dreams. In the scene where Costner's daughter is choking on a piece of hot dog, Lancaster must make the decision to stay on the field and remain in his fantasy or step over the line and save the child's life. By making the choice to save the child, he eliminates any chance of returning to the field. He chooses to step over the line and return to his present life. He then makes a statement, pointing out that he helped more people and done more good as a doctor than would have been possible as a major league baseball player.

Korcheck's decision to end his baseball career and alter the course of his life in some way parallels the movie scene in *Field of Dreams*. Korcheck decided to attend George Washington University in Washington D.C. He accepted a position as head baseball coach, and continued his studies toward a master's degree in education. The following year, Steve completed his doctoral degree in higher education administration. He moved to Sarasota,

Steve Korcheck

203

Florida in June and accepted a position with former major league player Sid Thrift, at the Kansas City Royals Baseball Academy. Two major leaguer players that graduated from the academy are Frank White and Oakland A's third base coach, Ron Washington.

In 1971 Steve accepted the position as professor of health education and assistant baseball coach at Manatee Junior College. The school continued to grow and gained the status of a full college. In 1976, he became the dean of Academic Affairs, and in 1980 Dr. Korcheck became the third president of Manatee College. He retired as president in 1987 after seventeen years of service.

Korcheck is like several players from the Fifties and Sixties who achieved more success after baseball in education, coaching, and other endeavors fields than they achieved on the baseball diamond. Korcheck is just one of them. Al Curtis and Dr. John Bagonzi are two others.

Curtis was born and raised, and still resides in Gaffney, South Carolina. He was an all-around athlete at Gaffney High School and excelling in baseball, football and basketball. Al signed a professional baseball contract with the Boston Red Sox,
and began his professional career as a pitcher, in Thomasville, Georgia.

We met for the first time in January of 1952 at a special spring training camp the Red Sox held for their top prospects. At the conclusion of that camp, Al and I were invited to join the major league team at spring training.

We played together at Louisville for the next couple of years, Curtis had all the tools to become a good major league pitcher and I believe the only thing that held him back was fate! He was a late starter; getting better as the season progressed, but by then someone else caught the eye of the Red Sox brass. Circumstances, being in the right place at the right time, never getting the right break were what denied him the opportunity to progress up the baseball latter, not his lack of ability.

After a few years Al decided to retire from baseball. He returned home, finished his education at Furman University and went on to become a teacher and one of the outstanding baseball and football coaches in South Carolina.

Bagonzi is another example of a player with quality ability who failed, for one reason or another, to achieve success in professional baseball. John, a left-handed pitcher, played high school baseball at Woodville High

204

School in New Hampshire, with another left- hand pitcher and roommate of mine with the Red Sox for several years, Bob Smith.

Bagonzi attended the University of New Hampshire where he set a number of college records, including five no-hitters. He signed with the Red Sox and spent several years in their minor league system and with the Chicago Cubs organization. "Russ, I wish I could have made the majors, but to be truthful I am just as pleased to have spent my talents in baseball teaching others to play, love, and understand the game of baseball," he said.

He earned a doctoral degree in kinesiology from Indiana University. He returned to New Hampshire to coach baseball at Woodsville High School where his teams registered over 700 victories, a winning percent-age of .830, and thirteen state championships.

Dr. Bagonzi has continued his commitment to baseball applying the science of kinesiology and how it applies to proper pitching mechanics. Coach Bagonzi operates his Championship Pitching Camps for high schools and colleges across the country and he has written a book, *The Art of Pitching*. He has received comments from many professional baseball stars such as Bob Feller. His book has gained a great deal of notice in baseball circles. Lennie Merullo, head of the New England Scouting Bureau said, "John is probably the finest pitching coach in the east — a pro's pro."

Clint Courtney, Catcher

Every major league team has its list of characters whose reputation precedes him when he moves from one team to another. Such was the case of Clinton Dawson Courtney, better known in baseball as "Scrap Iron." He was five-foot-eight and tipped the scales at 180 pounds of solid muscle.

The stories of his willingness to fight at the drop of a hat were legends. He would go into second base to break up a double play and come up swinging and when he tagged a runner out at home, they said he mugged him. He was truly a rebel from his southern birth in Louisiana to the playing fields of baseball. During his eleven-year major league career, the most he ever struck out in a season was 26. He was voted Rookie of the Year in the American League in 1952 as a member of the St. Louis Browns. He had a .286 batting average with 60 assists and only two errors.

Clint Courtney

He was a product of the New York Yankee farm system where he toiled for seven years before getting an opportunity with the Browns. Clint was the first catcher in baseball to ever wear glasses under his mask.

I had the experience of being a teammate of Courtney's with the Senators from 1957 through 1960. Clint went through some of the most noteworthy experiences of his career. His batting stroke will not go down in history as one of the picture swings in the game. In fact, Ted Williams thought it was so bad that he refused to watch him hit. But, he seldom struck out and always seemed to get the bat on the ball. He also had a respectable career batting average of .268. This should be a reminder that there is no one correct way to hit or play the game. Scraps, like the Sinatra song, did it his way.

Most of the Senator players rented apartments in one area of Alexandria, Virginia. Players would share rides to the ballpark and alternate cars during a home stay. Clint drove a Cadillac, a big four-door job. I wondered why he never drove his car until one day Hal Griggs suggested I look in the back seat. Man, I never saw so many beer cans in my life. Clint liked his beer and when he finished a can he would simply flip the empty into the back seat. The only problem was he seldom, if ever, took the time to clean up the mess in the back of the car. For all I know it may have stayed that way until he traded cars.

One year, Courtney had a mental block that made it impossible for him to throw the ball back to the pitcher after a pitch. Catchers normally like to fire the horsehide back to the pitcher with gusto, and pitchers like that because for one reason or another it fires us up. Clint tried everything anyone mentioned to try to end the predicament with the exception of rolling the ball back to the pitcher. It was bad enough with no one on base, but with runners on base it was like a fire drill. We finally tried having the first and third basemen break toward the pitchers mound with a man on first in case Clint's errant throw was off to the left or right. That didn't work because it was almost impossible for the first baseman to hold the runner close to the bag. Runners were stealing second running backwards. The next step was a gentle lob back to the pitcher. I actually believe that the delayed steal was developed at this time. Runners at first or second would wait until Scraps cocked his arm to release the ball and while it floated softly toward the mound would steal second or third.

In some ways, it reminded me of a Little League game the first year runners are permitted to take a lead and steal the next base. Perhaps it was more like a Chinese fire drill. The next and final stage before hypnosis was the just-fire-it-back-to-the-pitcher-and-the-hell with-where-it goes stage. During this attempt to solve Courtney's throwing problem, we developed more infielders and pitchers for gymnastics than the Olympic tryouts. I never witnessed so many unbelievable catches of a thrown ball since viewing a Circus act performed by a seal and an elephant when I was ten years old.

A sideward, headlong dive toward third or first with a backhanded catch between the legs was not out of the ordinary for the pitching staff. Nor was it unusual to see a second basemen or shortstop make a laid-out horizontal diving catch over second base, perform a tuck- and- roll maneuver and finish with a perfect two- footed landing while holding a runner to second base. The opposing teams gave us more perfect ten scores and the fans gave more standing ovations than were given in the history of the Washington franchise. Finally, those in charge, under the threat of a walkout by the pitchers and infielders, made the decision to change catchers until Scraps could find a way to solve his throwing problem.

Courtney's next stage was what we pitchers termed the multiple-sign-and-finger stage. Baseball fans, especially those who watch televised games are familiar with the view of the catcher giving hand signs to the pitcher. Today's signals are fairly complicated. The catcher may start the signs from his right leg, drop a finger or two, move to the left leg, go through a similar series on the right leg and finish with a fist in the center. Things were much more simplified in our day. If there were no base runners and a catcher wanted the pitcher to throw a fastball he simply put down one finger. If he wanted a curve he put down two. If he wanted a slider it was three fingers, and if he chose a changeup he would wiggle all his fingers.

However, we took precautions with a runner at second and went to multiple signs. These usually consisted of the catcher telling the pitcher to take the second sign in the series he would give. If the catcher put down one finger, followed by two fingers and again followed with three fingers, and he had told the pitcher to take the second sign, which in the example was two fingers, he was telling the pitcher to throw a curveball. Now all this seems simple enough except it was almost impossible to get through to Clint that a one-one-one signal was not a multiple sign since all the finger signs were the same finger, making it easy for a runner at second base to pick up. Clint really labored with finding a system the pitchers and he could agree on. I believe the pitching staff finally agreed among ourselves that we would throw whatever we wanted to and if it fooled Scraps and he didn't catch the pitch, so what, he'd lead the league in passed balls. Actually we finally found a system that both catcher and pitchers were comfortable with.

Now I've given you the impression that Scraps wasn't too smart but believe me that was not the case. He could not be cheated in a card game and in anything that involved money you had better make it right down to the penny. For some reason he just had trouble with finger signs.

Scraps also didn't have a great interest or concern for personal hygiene. He had a reputation of taking the shortest showers in the league. At times he walked through the shower using as little water as possible. He was usually dressed and was gone before most of us left the shower. Clint wore the same sweatshirt until it literally fell apart, then he would switch to the second shirt, and if by chance, it also fell apart before the season ended he would purchase another one. Scrap's health habits caused a few strange odors to hang around his locker as the baseball season moved into June and July. The players gentle kidding about the odors fell on deft ears, or perhaps the fact that Clint had a cattle ranch left him feeling comfortable with the smell. In any event there were times when it got a little ripe!

One day during a really hot week in Chicago, it was difficult to tell if the odors around Comiskey Park were from the wind blowing off the stockyards or from Courtney's locker. When several of the Chicago players mentioned the smell at home plate our bullpen catcher for the Sox, Les Moss, a prankster of utmost degree, decided to teach Scraps a lesson. He got Hal Griggs to get Courtney's glove from his locker after a game and give it too him.

Les opened the lacing on the heel of the glove and removed some of the padding and replaced it with Limburger cheese then retied the lacing. He returned the glove to the clubhouse man before batting practice, and he put it back in Clint's locker.

The heat index reached near a hundred and by the time Scraps warmed up and took infield practice, plus the ball pounding into the glove, had the cheese ready to ferment. Ed Runge was working the plate that afternoon and several of the Chicago players who were aware of the prank began to complain to Ed that the smell at home plate was a little strong. Along about the bottom of the third inning, Runge bellowed, "Play ball," and settled into position over Scraps left shoulder. The first pitch of the inning smacked into the glove and suddenly the smell hit Runge full tilt. He leaped away from the plate and called "Time." He then approached Clint and said, "Scraps, you smell like hell, what were you drinking last night?"

Clint just laughed. After a couple of more pitches, Ed could stand it no longer, once again he called time and walked over to the Senator dugout and approached manager Cookie Lavagetto. "Cookie, I don't know what Courtney's been drinking but he smells like horseshit," Runge declaired. "Get him to change his shirt after this inning or I'm going to throw him out of the game."

Cookie suggested that it was his own odor he smelled not Clint's, and Ed returned to the plate grumbling. By the next inning the real flavor of the cheese had reached it peak. As fate would have it, the inning happened to be one of those long drawn out deals with a lot of full counts and foul balls. By now the smell engulfed the Sox hitters and Runge both. The word quickly spread to both dugouts about the prank and both benches began to taunt Ed to throw Scraps out of the game. After the next out, Runge happened to look at Clint's glove and saw the cheese oozing out from the heel of the mitt and realized the source of the smell was the glove not Clint himself. Clint changed his shirt and borrowed a glove from one of the Senator catchers, which improved the smell at home plate, The fans wondered what was going on. The players had a great laugh that added a little inside humor to a hot afternoon in Chicago. You know, as I come to think back on that day it seemed to me that Scraps was the only one the smell didn't bother. Oh well, to each his own.

Joe Ginsberg, Catcher

Joe Ginsberg was one of the best receivers in the game of baseball and one of the nicest and more naturally humorous guys I have ever been around. Joe was a teammate of mine in Chicago. More importantly we are still good friends today, and see each other several times a year at golf outings in Florida and Indiana. Joe's major league career lasted 13 years.

Ginsberg tells more humorous stories than anyone in baseball with the

Joe Ginsberg

exception of Tommy Lasorda. He is in great demand at baseball reunions and especially old timer gatherings and golf outings. My favorite Ginsberg story involves Birdie Tebbetts, who was catching for the Red Sox when Joe came up with the Tigers. Detroit was in Boston for a Saturday afternoon game at Fenway Park. Along about the fifth inning, the Red Sox loaded the bases with one out. The first two pitches by the Tiger pitcher just missed outside. With the count 0-2, Tebbetts looked down at the third base coach to pick up a sign; hit away or take. Birdie grit his teeth and dropped his head in disgust. He began mumbling to himself, but loud enough for Joe and the umpire to hear him. "I'll be dammed. I've been in this league 10 years, played my share of games, got my share of big hits. Why in hell's name do they want me to take the 2-0 pitch? Hell, I guess they think I'll hit into a double play or something I just don't understand."

Birdie laid out a convincing story, good enough to talk Joe into calling for a fastball. The pitch was right down the middle. Joe heard the crack of the bat and watched as the grand-slam home run settled into the net above the "Green Monster" in left field.

The umpire just smiled at Ginsberg and said, "Kid, welcome to the big leagues. You learned a lesson today that you'll never forget." And I guess that Joe never did.

Ginsberg was an outstanding receiver with the skills and personality to handle pitchers and get the most out of them. He was a left-handed hitter who could handle the bat well in hit-run or bunt situations. Because of these skills he was a valuable asset to a team.

Joe played thirteen years in the major leagues with Detroit, Cleveland, Kansas City, Baltimore, and the White Sox in the American League and the New York Mets in the National League. His career batting average was .241 and his fielding average .980, a great average for a catcher.

Joe is one of my prime example of a Twinkling Star: long career, not overly impressive numbers, but with so many skills that he was a valuable asset to any team he played for, and always in demand.

Chapter 11
Life After Baseball

In late September 1963, Oklahoma City made its last trip of the season into Indianapolis. Ernie Andres, who had a brief stay as an infielder with the Red Sox, was the baseball coach at Indiana University. He came out to the ballpark to see me. I knew who Ernie was, but I had never met him.

After the game, we had dinner together and my future plans became the subject of our conversation. Ernie suggested that I come to Bloomington, Indiana as his assistant coach and finish my degree. This would enable me to pursue my interest in theology.

A few weeks later, I received a letter from Ernie informing me that arrangements had been made with Indiana University and the Methodist

Church to move us to Indianapolis. Details had been worked out allowing me to complete my degree, coach baseball at Indiana University, and work with the Methodist Church in some capacity. The changing situation in Houston made the decision easy. I accepted the offer from Indiana and bid a fond farewell to professional baseball.

The move to Indiana was exciting to say the least. My wife and I were brought up in a big-city environment. The change to Monrovia, Indiana and rural life was quite a change! We soon became acclimated to life in small town mid-America.

I enrolled at Indiana University and registered for the second semester that would begin in January. Baseball practice would start with a fall session in October and resume when classes began again in January.

The arrangements with the Methodist Church were more demanding! I needed to take a series of private classes directed toward achieving a Lay Pastors license permitting me to carry out all of the duties of a pastor. Several of the classes were correspondent courses through the seminary. Other classes were held at the Methodist Church office in Indianapolis.

My duties called for me to assume the operation of two churches in the area. The Monrovia Methodist Church, a congregation of 100 or more members, and the Salem Methodist Church, a congregation made up of elderly members, about 25 in number.

The Salem churches needs were rather basic. A sermon each Sunday morning, visitation, hospital calls, and emergency functions. The Monrovia church was more demanding! Duties included Sunday messages, visitations, hospital calls, home visitations, weddings, funerals, and a youth program. I was overloaded, especially when class at Indiana began in January. My school schedule called for classes on Monday, Wednesday, and Friday. Two days were spent preparing for Sundays and one day and evenings reading, writing papers, and helping with the family. When baseball practice began in earnest my schedule became more demanding. All in all, I was as busy as a one-armed paper-hanger.

For example, I recall a dinner program for the ladies had been scheduled for an evening I was to be at the university attending a required lecture. I knew I'd be rushed to get back in time, so I set up the tables and made sure all the arrangements were made, and those in the program reminded of their duties. I asked my wife to find something colorful to use as table decorations and headed to the university.

I returned home shortly before the program started and admired the centerpieces that stood out on each table. They were small baskets filled with beautiful colored leaves, plentiful, and in abundance, this season of the year. My wife, children, and several of the neighborhood children, hand picked the leaves and helped Betty arrange them in baskets.

The program was moving along quite well until midway through the evening one of the ladies identified the leaves. They were poison ivy! The festivities came to a screeching halt as mothers grabbed their children and raced home to find grandma's remedy for the itching.

I was sorry to report that most of the adults and all of the children in the congregation, including my wife and two of our own, came down with the worst case of poison ivy the community had ever seen! There was talk of evacuating the school until someone realized poison ivy wasn't couldn't be carried from person to person.

I felt so sorry for Betty! She was labeled, "the poor preacher's city-girl-wife who didn't know a poison ivy leaf from a rose petal." That was the nice thing that was said.

I was so rushed at times to prepare a Sunday message I thought of using taped messages. In desperation, I reached for copies of messages I had saved as reference material. There was one series of four sermons entitled, *The Church in Difficult Days*, I thought was outstanding, I had listened to Dr. Smith preach the series in Bloomington Illinois, when I was helping at his church. I felt with a little revision I could use these messages and save me hours of study, research, and assure the quality of the message.

It never occurred to me that the age differences in the two congregations might require more detailed adjustments, or that an affluent congregation in a college town, such as Bloomington, would be more in tune with Dr. Smith's level of sermon than a small town in Indiana.

The first sermon in the series was entitled, "Sex, Sinners, and Saints." The sermon was mildly received by the Monrovia congregation, which was predominantly still in the child bearing age. The Salem congregation, with an average age of 75, considerably beyond having any interest sexual sermons, received the message in stunned silence! After the service an elderly gentleman took my hand, looked up into my eyes and expressed himself from the heart. "Son, I'm 83 years old, and I declare, that's the worst sermon I have ever heard in my life!" I didn't know whether to break out in laughter or cry, but it did teach me a valuable lesson about public speaking. Know your audience!

Another experience took place in the Monrovia church. One of the members of the congregation passed away and left a small sum of money use for improvements to the building. Rather than have the church board make the decision of how to use the money I suggested that we have a short meeting following the Sunday morning worship service to allow the congregation to offer suggestions followed by discussion.

When I asked for suggestions, a young women stood and said, "I would like to suggest we purchase a chandelier for the sanctuary." I then asked if there was any discussion? An elderly gentleman stood up and expressed himself. "I'm against it. I'm against it. I'm against it for three reasons! First, I don't know of anyone in this town that can play one of those things! Secondly, it's so dog-gone big I don't know where we would put the darn thing! And third, I believe what we really need in this church is a light for the ceiling!" End of discussion, we purchased the chandelier.

Early in January, following the holiday break, baseball practice moved into full-swing in the fieldhouse, which was a large, barrack-building with a dirt floor. The facility housed the basketball court and stands, but there was still plenty of room for several batting and pitching cages — a make shift infield.

We were really hurting for space until the home basketball season was over and the basketball court and bleachers taken down. One problem still remained. The low structure of the fieldhouse, along with inadequate lighting, made it impossible to hit fly balls to the outfielder or pop-ups to the infield. The spring weather in Indiana seldom permitted us to practice outdoors. When the team headed to Texas in late March, we had to practice every morning hitting fly balls to the team. Until we had a few practices and a couple of games under our belts our kids look like monkeys chasing a football in a windstorm.

Andres proved to be a great friend! He fit the image of a retired jock to the "T." I had more fun with him during my three years at Indiana than at anytime since I was playing summer baseball in Pittsburgh. I would describe him as being a high-strung, serious type person. He certainly was a knowledgeable coach with a personality that attracted people.

The baseball team traveled on road trips on one of the universities DC-3 airplanes. The plane was small, restricting us from taking the full team on road trips. One of my duties was to check out a van from the university car pool, load up with the extra reserve players, and drive to the game. Normally we left the campus early on Friday morning, depending upon the distance we had to travel.

Ernie was a nervous wreck until we arrived. He was like a mother hen worrying about her chicks. We usually carried the load of the baseball equipment in the van, and the thought of us not arriving in time for the game and having to use the other teams equipment was a constant worry.

After the single game on Friday the team would have dinner together at a local establishment, and the kids were on their own until curfew, usually at 11 p.m.. Ernie would check and recheck the rooms several times a night to make sure the kids were in their rooms. I'm not sure if it was the kids he mistrusted or his awareness of all the things players did in pro-baseball to beat the dreaded curfew.

Ernie was not a sleeper! What I mean is, he worried so much about the players, if they were prepared, if it would rain, who to play and not play. The list went on and on usually resulting in him getting me up at 3 a.m. to go get a cup of coffee or to check the players rooms one more time. After being with him for three years, I didn't sleep much more than he did.

One method used to check rooms was to call and talk to each of the two players assigned to the room. We happened to have a young man on the team who had a mild speech impediment, he stuttered. On one road trip Ernie called the room well after curfew, and the player with the impediment answered the phone. Ernie asked, "John is that you?" The reply came back, "Ya yass, yes sir it, it its ma, ma me!"

Andres replied, "Let me speak to Billy."

"Co-co coach, he, he he's in the sho, sho, shower."

"John, you go get him and tell him I want to speak with him now, and I mean now!"

In a few seconds a voice answered, "Co,co coach, Thi thi this, is Bi, bil, Billy."

Ernie was laughing so hard tears were rolling down his cheeks. He just handed me the phone and said, "Coach see if this sounds like Billy to you?" Needless to say, both John and Billy had more than a few extra laps to run prior to the game the next day. Billy for breaking curfew and John for covering up for Billy.

One other thing that haunted Andres was superstitions. He always insisted on taking the same route to the field everyday at home or away. He would wear the same shirt, eat the same breakfast, and go through the same routine.

One Saturday we were scheduled to play a double-header at home with Taylor University. Usually, playing a non-Big-Ten school was easy pickings. But Taylor had a good ball club with solid pitching. Coach had two rituals he went through before every game. First, he would give the team a short pep talk. Secondly, he would always go into the small restroom at the end of the dugout and smoke a cigarette.

I decided I would deliver the pep talk. "Men, you have all heard the saying, it's not whether you win or lose, but how you play the game. Well that's a bunch of bull! Now go out there and kick the crap out of them!"

Well, Taylor beat us in both ends of the double-header. Ernie went around mumbling all week. "I didn't bring you here to give the damn pet talks. It's not whether you win or lose. That's a bunch of bull!" On and on he would go. He never allowed me to give a pep talk the rest of the time I was at Indiana.

One day we were playing Iowa at home. Ernie always coached third base, but like I said, he was superstitious. Along about the third inning things were not going well for the Hoosiers. Following another futile time at bat coach came into the dugout with steam blowing from every pour. "You take it next inning. Hell I ain't doing any good. You must have given them another pep talk or something!" He went right into the outhouse at the end of the dugout. He was still there when we came to bat in out half of the inning.

As fate would have it we got hot. A hit, walk, error, followed by a base hit and we had a rally going. I walked over to the dugout while Iowa was changing pitchers and set the pad lock on the outside of the door, locking Ernie inside.

The rally continued and soon an angry voice could be heard coming from our dugout. "Open this damn door! Open it I say!" Ernie's plea fell on deaf ears! Even when we returned to the field, I wouldn't open the door. In fact, I wouldn't even talk to him except to tell him we had a rally going so just smoke another butt. His cussing and banging got the attention of the umpires, who approached me to find out what all the fuss was about. When I explained the situation, they just laughed and went back to their positions.

Three innings later I unlatched the door. Ernie was hot! He called me everything that came to mind including a threat to sending me back to Oklahoma City. We won that game with Iowa and followed it with four wins in a row. He never let me coach third again, even when we were losing. You might say he was superstitious, or he was afraid of being locked in the outhouse again.

The old saying is that time passes quickly when your having a good time. It certainly was true of my days at Indiana University and my relationship with coach Ernie Andres.

Soon after receiving my park and recreation degree from Indiana, I accepted a position as Park and Recreation Director in Seymour, Indiana. The family gathered our belonging and headed south, where we resided for the next seven years. We had all grown accustomed to life in small town and liked it!

The responsibility of directing the recreation program kept me extremely busy during the spring and summer months. Two parks in the city housed various activities from morning to 11 p.m. each evening except Sunday. We termed it our cradle-to-grave activities program because it covered all ages. We had instructional classes in crafts, swimming, tennis, volleyball, softball, baseball leagues for boys and American Legion baseball for junior and senior boys. It was a full-time program and demanded my full attention.

And just in case all this wasn't enough, I took on the full-time responsibility of being a part-time pastor at the United Church of Christ. I was asked to be the guest speaker soon after our arrival in town. I also requested to become a temporary pastor until a full-time replacement could be found. Seven years later I was still a temporary pastor.

Along about this time there was a political change in town that replaced the mayor that hired me. Park and recreation departments are not politically motivated in any sense of the word, but when the new mayor took office I was replaced. About this time in my life that I realized I missed the challenge of an athletic life. I wanted to coach and teach full time. I had coached junior football and organized baseball clinics, but I felt a need to get into teaching and coaching as a full-time profession.

I decided to return to Indiana University and work toward a secondary education degree with an emphasis on English. It took me the about 18 months to earn the necessary credits for my degree. Now came the tough job or finding a school corporation willing to take a chance on an over-40 retired pro baseball player with little teaching experience.

A friend of mine and football coach, Dick Ranard, persuaded his superintendent to hire me as the junior high football coach and an assistant high school coach. My responsibility was teaching six classes of seventh grade English, coaching the Junior High football team, and working with Ranard during the high school football games.

I was in a hurry to find a permanent place because I was twenty years older than the coaches on most high school staffs, and I felt opportunities would be limited because of my age. I was told of an opening in the town of Milan, Indiana, which was close to Cincinnati. I applied and got the job as football coach and junior high English teacher.

Milan was a basketball town. The school was the last small high school in Indiana to win the boys state basketball championship and the movie "Hoosiers" was based on its success. That was nearly 50 years ago. The football team had not won a game in two years. It appeared that this was the perfect spot to begin my football head- coaching career. Little would be expected and there would be little pressure to win.

We won our first two games and one more toward the end of the season. It was the best record in ten years. Considering Milan had a combined enrollment of 300 in junior and senior high school, and were playing against school with three to five times that enrollment, it was a remarkable record. We won three and lost seven and things looked a little better for next year.

My second season we improved to four and six, but there was serious discussion that the school board was considering suspending football because of the size of the enrollment and the difficulty of scheduling schools our size. One thing was certain, this was not the school I wanted to spend the rest of my teaching and coaching career at. With the uncertainty of the football program and the realization that I needed to find a high school in a large metropolitan area if I wanted to coach baseball, I began to look for possibilities.

The following July, I accepted a position as head baseball and assistant football coach with a teaching position in the English department at Lawrence Central High School, one of three high schools, in the Metropolitan School District of Lawrence Township, located on the east side of Indianapolis. The next nineteen years of my life would be lived in this building and on the athletic fields outside.

I would meet and marry my second wife, Susannah K. Kemmerer. My first wife had passed away as a result of Lou Gehrig's Disease or also known as ALS. I would learn to appreciate the privilege of working with a superb faculty, administrators, coaches, parents and students. I would realize in a variety of ways, the value of education and experience unnumbered times over, the thrill of seeing the lights turned on for a multitude of students. I would get to understand the depth of teaching when graduating students returned to relate in affectionate words, how you and other teachers had helped them hammer out the important decisions in their lives. And I remember the little perks given in respect, such as a nickname fashioned by the students for me, "Special K." And a ton of memories, victories, and defeats.

I was once asked if I would rather be remembered, as a major league player or a teacher? That's a tough question because I love the game of baseball. I always have, it's been a part of my life as long as I can remember. But I remember the first time I saw the light of knowledge turn on in a young man's eyes. I was trying to explain a rather simple concept in English, the agreement of subject and verb in a sentence. The young man had missed every one of the twenty sentences on the quiz. With painstaking patience, I began to search for the key that would open his mind and permit him to understand the concept.

I saw that light come on many times in the twenty-three years I taught and coached. I can't tell you the untold number of times students have sought me out long after graduation, to thank me for understanding, and reaching out when their lives seemed difficult. Something I did or said righted their sinking ship and helped them move through the problem and get on with their lives. I wouldn't trade anything for those moments. I believe the choice is simple. I'd rather be remembered as a teacher/coach, a God-fearing man, who in some small way was able to reach out and touch his fellow man in a positive way.

I still get my share of autograph and picture requests from baseball fans that collect memorabilia, sometimes as many as twenty or thirty a month. The subject they are most curious about is what was my greatest thrill in baseball? I had my share of thrills. I've had my share of highlights, but it's not the thrills or highlights I cherish most — it's baseball, the game and the men I played with and against. Most fans cherish a picture, an autograph, a handshake, or a special passing moment with their hero.

I lived baseball with these players, and knew them as great athletes. More importantly, I know them as successful people, businessmen, dedicated husbands, fathers, grandparents, community leaders, and down to earth God-fearing men. Beyond their athletic achievements on the baseball diamond lies a quality most of them would reluctantly acknowledge, the influence, either directly or indirectly, on the lives of untold numbers of fans that list them as idols and heroes.

I lived the game then, I live it now, and I will continue to live it, and share it, until the Great Scorer places the final tally beside my name in the big scorebook of life!

Here I am with my Lawrence Central High School team, which won the sectional championship in 1980.

Appendix I
Statistics

YEAR	TEAM	LEAGUE	G	IP	W	L	PCT	SO	BB	ERA
1951	Scranton	Eastern	5	21	0	1	.000	9	10	4.20
1951	Roanoke	Piedmont	35	167	6	11	.353	99	118	4.69
1952	Louisville	A.A.	25	126	7	8	.467	69	62	5.43
1953	Louisville	A.A.	34	188	11	8	.579	109	81	3.40
1954	Louisville	A.A.	14	104	5	6	.455	55	44	1.08
1954	Boston	A.L.	19	75	5	3	.625	37	41	3.84
1955	Boston	A.L.	7	17	1	1	.500	13	15	7.41
1955	Louisville	A.A.	28	118	3	8	.273	46	49	4.96
1956	San Fran.	P.C.L.	38	233	12	14	.462	137	93	3.48
1957	Bost.-Wash.	A.L.	40	176	7	11	.389	82	73	4.96
1958	Washington	A.L.	40	224	6	15	.286	111	74	4.62
1959	Washington	A.L.	37	206	8	17	.320	89	71	4.50
1960	Wash.-Chi.	A.L.	39	138	6	5	.545	86	55	3.59
1961	Chicago	A.L.	47	97	3	3	.500	35	26	4.38
1962	Chicago	A.L.	20	28	2	1	.667	17	11	3.86
1962	Houston	N.L.	36	68	5	3	.625	23	15	4.10
1963	Houston	N.L.	17	36.2	0	0	.000	12	8	5.65
1963	Ok. City	P.C.L.	21	74	5	3	.625	45	21	2.80
ML Totals										
9 yrs			302	1067	43	59	.422	505	189	4.46
Career Totals										
12 yrs			502	2097	92	118	.438	1074	882	4.31

NOTE: Rus also had two shutouts and 8 saves in the majors. His win-loss record as a reliever was 18-7. His batting average was .128 with two homers. He also had a fielding average of .944.

Appendix II
Ted Williams Museum

The last time I saw Ted Williams was at his own museum, The Ted Williams Museum and Hitters Hall of Fame, during the 9th annual induction ceremony in 2002. It was an amazing event. One of the greatest highlights of the ceremony was when Ted made an unexpected appearance. His son, John Henry gave a moving tribute to his legendary father that brought many in the audience to tears, including myself. Many of the players honored were present to receive their awards. Dwight Evans, the family of Roger Maris, Don Mattingly, Cal Ripken, Jr., and Enos Slaughter were all here for their induction. Gaylord Perry and Virgil Trucks were honored on our Wall of Great Achievement, and the year's Most Productive Hitter, Jason Giambi, was in attendance to receive his award. Al Kaline was also present to receive the 3,000 Hit Club Award. Dwight Gooden accepted on behalf of the Splendid Splinter award winner, Derek Jeter, and Rookie of the Year for the American League, Alfonso Soriano. The Master of Ceremonies Tommy Lasorda, who thrilled the crowd with his colorful stories and paid tribute to many of the heroes.

Inductees to Date

Aaron, Hank	1995		Maris, Roger	2002
Banks, Ernie	1998		Mathews, Eddie	1998
Bench, Johnny	2000		Mattingly, Don	2002
Berra, Yogi	1999		Mays, Willie	1995
Brett, George	2000		McCovey, Willie	1996
Clemente, Roberto	2000		Mize, Johnny	1995
Cobb, Ty	1995		Molitor, Paul	2001
DiMaggio, Joe	1995		Musial, Stan	1995
Evans, Dwight	2002		Oh, Sadaharu	1999
Fisk, Carlton	2000		Ott, Mel	1995
Foxx, Jimmie	1995		Rice, Jim	2001
Gehrig, Lou	1995		Ripken, Jr., Cal	2002
Gibson, Josh	1996		Robinson, Frank	1995
Greenberg, Hank	1995		Ruth, Babe	1995
Heilmann, Harry	1995		Schmidt, Mike	1995
Hornsby, Rogers	1995		Simmons, Al	1995
Jackson, Joe	1998		Slaughter, Enos	2002
Jackson, Reggie	1998		Snider, Duke	1996
Kaline, Al	1999		Speaker, Tris	1995
Killebrew, Harmon	1996		Stargell, Willie	1999
Kiner, Ralph	1995		Winfield, Dave	2001
Klein, Chuck	1996		Yastrzemski, Carl	1999
Leonard, Buck	1998		Yount, Robin	2001
Mantle, Mickey	1995			

I joined Virgil Trucks (left) and Tommy Lasorda for a photo at the Ted Williams Museum.

That's me with Johnny Pesky at the Ted Williams Museum.

Bibliography

The Baseball Encyclopedia, New York, NY: Macmillian Publishing Co., 1993, Ninth Edition.

Brace Photo, Chicago, IL

Egan, Dave, *Boston Globe*, July 21, 1954.

Gough, David, *They've Stolen Our Team: 1947*, Alexandria, VA: D.L. Megbec Publishing.

Gough, David, *Nats News*, Washington Historical Baseball Society, Spring 1999, Vol. #12.

Helyar, *Lord of The Realm*, New York, NY: Villard Books.

Vincent, David, *SABR News*, Woodbridge, VA.

Williams, Pat with Michael Weinreb, *Marketing Your Dreams,* Champaign, IL: Sports Publishing, Inc., 2000.

Wood, Phil, *Nats News*, Washington Historical Baseball Society, Fall 1999, Vol #14.

Baseball Programs:
Boston Red Sox, 1955
Washington Senators, 1957
Chicago White Sox, 1961

Index